French Naval Aviation

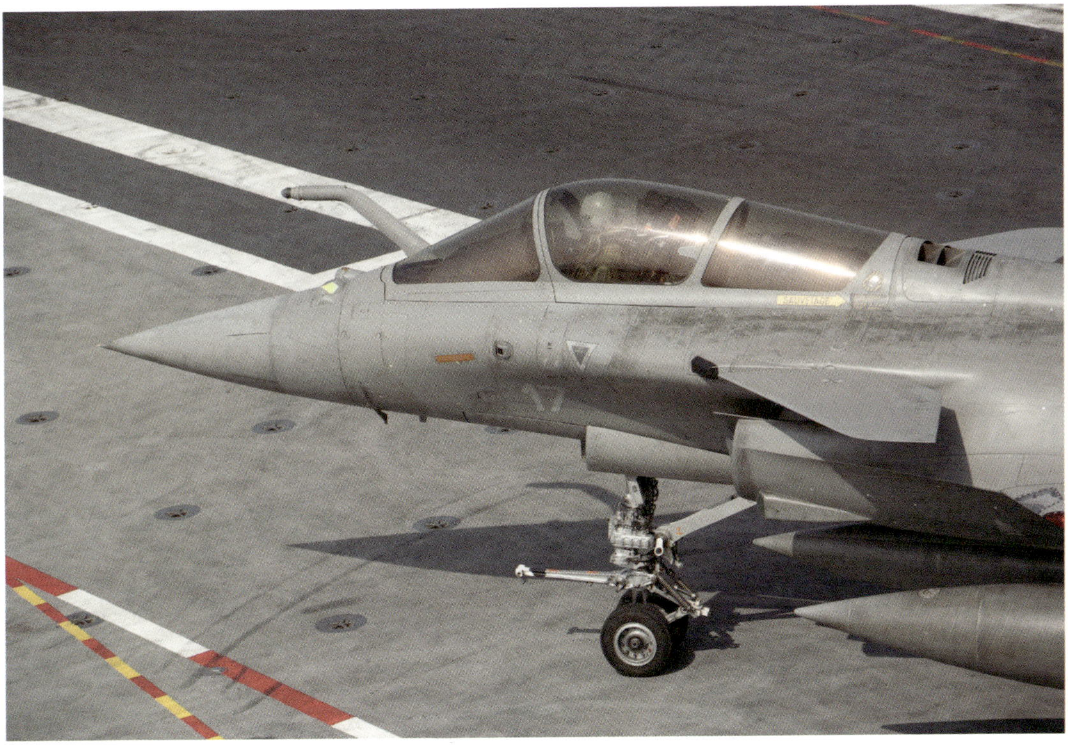

HENRI-PIERRE GROLLEAU

Key Books

MODERN MILITARY AIRCRAFT SERIES, VOLUME 7

Front cover image: The Rafale M fighter fleet forms the tip of the spear of the Aéronautique Navale.

Back cover image: The Atlantique 2 maritime patrol aircraft is currently undergoing a major upgrade programme.

Title page image: A Rafale M is marshalled towards its parking spot after trapping on board nuclear carrier *Charles de Gaulle*.

Contents page image: A Flottille 4F E-2C Hawkeye comes in to land on board *Charles de Gaulle*. The E-2C will be replaced by the more modern E-2D.

Acknowledgements

The author would like to thank all military and civilian personnel for the invaluable assistance provided during his various reports over the years, at the Landivisiau, Lanvéoc-Poulmic, Lann-Bihoué and Hyères naval air stations, and on board carrier *Charles de Gaulle* and frigates *Forbin* and *Latouche-Tréville*: Admiral Vandier, Admiral Janicot, Captains Berling, Dumont-Dayot, Lavault, Moreau and Turret, Captain Marc, Commanders Lallouet, Madec, Franck and Thierry, Lieutenant-Commanders Archambeaud, Féraud, Gonnot, Wertenberg, Olivier, Thomas and Jacques, Lieutenants Emilie and Nicoles, Midships Caroline and Pacôme, and Mrs Duboc.

Published by Key Books
An imprint of Key Publishing Ltd
PO Box 100
Stamford
Lincs PE19 1XQ

www.keypublishing.com

The right of Henri-Pierre Grolleau to be identified as the author of this book has been asserted in accordance with the Copyright, Designs and Patents Act 1988 Sections 77 and 78.

Copyright © Henri-Pierre Grolleau, 2022

All photographs are the copyright of Henri-Pierre Grolleau.

ISBN 978 1 80282 195 6

All rights reserved. Reproduction in whole or in part in any form whatsoever or by any means is strictly prohibited without the prior permission of the Publisher.

Typeset by SJmagic DESIGN SERVICES, India.

Contents

Foreword 4

Chapter 1   A Powerful, Agile and Multirole Force 6

Chapter 2   Aircrew Selection and Training 12

Chapter 3   Carrier Aviation 28

Chapter 4   Navy Helicopters at Sea 50

Chapter 5   Maritime Patrol and Maritime Surveillance 68

Chapter 6   SAR Missions 90

Foreword

Over the last 20 years, the Aéronautique Navale (French Naval Aviation) has evolved from a Cold War-era force, which flew a fleet of ageing aircraft, to a powerful, agile, flexible, battle-hardened force equipped with the latest generation of fixed-wing and helicopter types. Gone are the classic F-8P Crusader interceptor, the sleek Étendard IVPM recce bird, the yellow-painted Rallye trainer, the carrier-borne propeller-driven Br.1050 Alizé anti-submarine aircraft, the multirole Nord 262 maritime surveillance twin, the massive SA 321 Super Frelon rescue helicopter, the legendary Super Étendard strike fighter, and the iconic Lynx submarine hunter. Thanks to huge investments, all these types have given way to more lethal and better-connected types, such as the E-2C Hawkeye airborne early warning aircraft, the Rafale Marine omnirole fighter, the NFH90 Caïman Marine multirole naval helicopter and the Standard 6 variant of the Br.1150 Atlantique 2 maritime patrol aircraft (MPA). New types are on the horizon, and the days of the few remaining 'Jurassic' airframes, such as the popular SA 319 Alouette III, are now numbered. An interim fleet of SA 365 Dauphins and H160 rotorcraft is to be flown until the H160M Guépard is delivered in sufficient numbers. The Albatros maritime surveillance aircraft will replace ageing Falcon 50Ms and

A pair of Rafale M fighters flying in a very tight formation. Modellers will note the difference in colours between the two aircraft.

Gardians. Looking further ahead, it has officially been confirmed that the E-2D Advanced Hawkeye will replace the E-2C Hawkeye later this decade, providing even better long-range, multi-domain, beyond-the-horizon detection capabilities.

French helicopters and aircraft operate on all seas and oceans, from the *Charles de Gaulle* nuclear carrier, from surface combatants, from support vessels and from French and foreign naval air stations and air bases. They actively participate in sovereignty missions around French overseas territories. Over the years, the Aéronautique Navale has accrued extensive combat experience and developed extremely robust operational procedures. Since the beginning of the intervention in Afghanistan, in late 2001, French Naval Aviation assets have been continuously engaged in combat operations in Afghanistan, Libya, Syria, and even deep in the Sahara, where Atlantique 2 MPAs carry out surveillance, intelligence and kinetic/close air support missions. Carrier fighters have destroyed countless terrorist hideouts and struck high-end targets in Libya, including radar, air bases, command posts, surface-to-air systems, artillery emplacements, and armoured vehicles. Helicopters are busy protecting French interests at sea (performing drug interdiction missions and human trafficking/illegal immigration control) and carrying out search and rescue (SAR) missions in daring conditions. They also spend considerable time practising anti-submarine warfare tactics alongside Atlantique 2s and protecting nuclear submarines as they both leave and return to their bases, while Falcon 50M and Gardian maritime surveillance aircraft keep a watchful eye on all shipping in areas of interest.

Henri-Pierre Grolleau

A Flottille 36F Panther Standard 2 hovering at very low-level over the Mediterranean Sea.

Chapter 1

A Powerful, Agile and Multirole Force

Within the French Armed Forces, the Aéronautique Navale plays a key role in carrying out defensive and offensive missions at sea and overland.

The Aéronautique Navale is the largest naval aviation in Europe. It is split into three main components:

- the carrier air wing, which includes the three Rafale naval squadrons based at Landivisiau, Brittany; the E-2C Hawkeye flottille stationed in Lann-Bihoué, Brittany; the Dauphin helicopters that specialise in plane guard duties; and a Caïman detachment that now deploys from the *Charles de Gaulle* nuclear carrier.
- the helicopter force, divided into various flottilles that field Caïman, Panther, Dauphin and Alouette III helicopters from naval bases in Lanvéoc-Poulmic, Brittany, and Hyères, in the south of France, and from detachments in French overseas territories.
- the maritime patrol/maritime surveillance force, which is split into the Atlantique 2, Falcon 50M (both centralised in Lann-Bihoué) and Gardian multi-engine aircraft based in the Pacific.

They are supported in their missions by a small number of training units and an operational evaluation unit, the Centre d'Expérimentations Pratiques et de Réception de l'Aéronautique Navale/Escadrille 10S (CEPA/10S, the French Navy operational evaluation centre), which handles a large quantity of trial programmes each year.

Strong commitment
Admiral Eric Janicot, Commander of the Aéronautique Navale explained:

France has the second largest maritime domain in the world, after the US, and the country devotes a large amount of resources to ensure that its sovereignty over that domain is fully respected. As part of this policy, France is committed to operating a large naval force from naval bases in continental France and in French overseas territories. In an era of great power competition, tensions have appeared in a number of regions, including the South China Sea, the Persian Gulf, the Eastern Mediterranean Sea and the Gulf of Guinea. All these areas of tensions have one thing in common, the sea. To protect its interests, France routinely deploys surface combatants and submarines to hotspots to show the flag and reaffirm its commitment to adhere to international treaties and enforce international laws. In order to do so, the Marine Nationale [French Navy] needs to maintain a strong naval force and a strong naval aviation that can operate from ships and/or from naval air stations and forward air bases. On top of its flagship, nuclear aircraft carrier *Charles de Gaulle* and her powerful carrier air group, the Marine Nationale operates a large fleet of nuclear ballistic submarines, nuclear attack submarines, surface combatants, amphibious warfare ships, mine warfare ships, ocean-going patrol vessels and support vessels. A large proportion of its surface ships are aviation capable, requiring an ever-increasing inventory of fixed-wing and rotary assets, including a growing number of unmanned aerial vehicles. The number of nations that operate submarines is also increasing and the quality of their submarines is on the rise, meaning that we must ensure that we field enough maritime patrol aircraft and anti-submarine helicopters to address the problem.

Intensive training
In this context of escalating tensions, the level of training of aircrews, technicians and support staff must be preserved in the long term. Admiral Janicot continued:

The French Navy works hard to maintain perishable skills at sea and our aircrews are trained to very high standards. Since the beginning of the crisis in Bosnia, in the early 1990s, they have been engaged more or less continuously in all sorts of combat operations and have developed advanced tactics that have proved highly effective, including during high-intensity combat operations in Kosovo and in Libya. Today, we have to make sure that we remain fully capable of conducting and sustaining high intensity operations in the high seas. We really want to maintain our blue water combat capabilities, because we might have to use them in the future. Therefore, we regularly train to attack naval forces at sea and fight off hostile submarines, as it is essential to practise in order to remain proficient. It is extremely hard to find frigates or destroyers at sea in bad weather if the vessels remain silent, with their radars and radios switched off. You really need to devote a large quantity of assets to find them. The most complicated thing is to sort out military warships from dense civilian shipping, when dozens of tankers, trawlers, cargoes and dhows sail in a small area. It is quite easy to find a raw radar return, but much harder to make sure who is who. It proves tricky to identify military vessels without entering their missile engagement zones. This is why training

A Flottille 31F Caïman returns to its Hyères home base at the end of a training sortie.

proves vital and why anti-ship tactics must be regularly rehearsed. Aircrews must practise, using all the means at their disposal, including electronic warfare. They rely on their threat libraries to identify radar types and warship classes. If enemy radars and radios are switched off, aircrews have to closely monitor their own radar contacts to determine hostile intentions. Anti-submarine warfare is another field that requires constant attention and regular practice to stay current and retain skills. Thankfully, we do not have difficulties maintaining the number of flight hours and the level of aircrew training.

French Naval Aviation aircraft, bases and units

Types	Bases	Units	Numbers
Rafale M	Landivisiau	Flottilles 11F, 12F, 17F	
	Saint-Dizier	ETR	44
	Istres	CEPA	
E-2C Hawkeye	Lann-Bihoué	Flottille 4F	3
Atlantique 2	Lann-Bihoué	Flottilles 21F and 23F	22
Falcon 50	Lann-Bihoué	Flottille 24F	8
Gardian	Tahiti / Nouméa	Flottille 25F	5
Caïman	Hyères / Lanvéoc	Flottilles 31F and 33F	27
Panther	Hyères	Flottille 36F	16
Dauphin N	Hyères / Le Touquet / La Rochelle	Flottille 35F	6
Dauphin N3+	Tahiti	Flottille 35F	2
Dauphin Pedro	Hyères	Flottille 35F	3
Dauphin N3	Lanvéoc / Hyères	Flottilles 34F and 35F	17 (loaned)
H160	*from 2023*	*Flottille 32F*	*6 (loaned)*
Alouette III	Lanvéoc	Flottille 34F	8
Xingu	Lann-Bihoué	Flottille 28F	11
Falcon 10	Landivisiau	Escadrille 57S	6
CAP 10	Lanvéoc	Escadrille 50S	5 + 2
SR20	Lanvéoc	Escadrille 50S	3 (loaned)

Below left: An Atlantique 2 Standard 5 climbs out of its Lann-Bihoué home base. The Atlantique 2 is a highly successful design.

Below right: A pair of Flottille 11F Rafale M omnirole fighters initiate a climb off the south coast of Brittany.

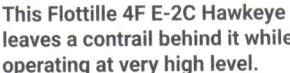

Above: Aircraft carrier *Charles de Gaulle* photographed during carrier qualifications. Nuclear propulsion has proved to be the right choice, giving the vessel unlimited endurance and excellent operational flexibility.

Right: The pilot of Rafale M41 has just started his two M88-2 turbofans. He will soon be catapulted away on a training mission.

This Flottille 4F E-2C Hawkeye leaves a contrail behind it while operating at very high level.

Above left: The Euroflir™ 410 EO turret is clearly visible on this photo of a Flottille 36F Panther Standard 2.

Above right: The E-2C Hawkeye is a surprisingly agile aircraft. Here, the first French Navy Hawkeye breaks away from the photo ship.

Above left: A Flottille 31F NH90 Caïman at very low level over the Mediterranean Sea.

Above right: A Flottille 34F Dauphin N3 overflies multi-mission frigate *Aquitaine* (D650) off Brittany, in 2019.

Below: The sleek lines of the Falcon 50 are clearly visible on this photo of aircraft serial number (s/n) 30 of Flottille 24F.

A Powerful, Agile and Multirole Force

An Escadrille 57S Falcon 10 at low-level over northern Brittany. The squadron specialises in the light transport/VVIP transportation role. It also provides instrument flying training to Rafale pilots.

Above: Flottille 34F will be equipped with a mixed fleet of Dauphin N3 and Alouette III helicopters until the latter is withdrawn from use in late 2022.

Below: The French Navy is slated to operate a growing number of unmanned aerial vehicles (UAV). Here, the demonstrator is the VSR700 UAV.

Chapter 2
Aircrew Selection and Training

The Aéronautique Navale devotes a lot of resources to aircrew selection, grading and training.

The French Navy has always been renowned for the quality of the training provided to its aircrews. It is fair to say that Étendard, Crusader and Super Étendard pilots trapping on board the rather small 32,000-tonne *Clemenceau* and *Foch* aircraft carriers had to rigorously adhere to procedures to avoid hitting their ramps or crashing onto their flight decks. To fly such demanding aircraft at night and in all weathers, pilots had to be carefully selected and trained to very high standards. Today, the French Navy still adheres to strict selection and grading standards and its fast jets, helicopters and multi-engine aircraft aircrews all follow long and arduous courses to become fully operational. The goal is not only for them to fly advanced aircraft and helicopters, but also to be able to operate in highly complex environments, as part of fully integrated combined and joint forces.

Aircrew selection

From Lanvéoc-Poulmic, Escadrille 50S operates a fleet of five Mudry CAP 10C basic trainers and three Cirrus SR20 light aircraft for the in-flight selection of future pilots. Two new CAP 10 NG (New Generation) trainers were ordered in late 2020 to bolster the inventory.

In the French Navy, pilots are either career officers graduating from the Ecole navale (Naval Academy), or direct entrant, short-commission officers. Whether they are interested or not in pursuing a career as a naval aviation pilot, all Naval Academy students log one sortie in the Cirrus to give them the opportunity to discover what it is like to fly. Among them, those who wish to become naval aviators fly up to five additional sorties in the Cirrus as part of a military aviation familiarisation course. The best individuals will fly a short course on the CAP 10C to screen those with the best abilities to become pilots. On average, 12 Naval Academy students are selected each year to become pilots.

Direct entrant officers join the French Navy after a thorough selection process that includes an in-depth medical examination and sporting, English-language and psycho-technical tests. Each year, anywhere between 45 and 50 students are allowed to undergo a grading process within Escadrille 50S, flying the CAP 10C. The syllabus includes 14 hours dual flight time with an instructor to assess the capabilities of the 'would-be pilots'. The trainees face a steep learning curve, with the syllabus following traditional military training lines: it comprises basic flying skills, circuit training, navigation, spinning and basic aerobatics. To progress beyond this stage, all trainees are required to successfully pass a final handling test. They are all issued with a military flight memento they must learn by heart. This manual gives them a detailed description of the sorties, and what to expect from the instructors. Apart from the first two sorties, each mission is marked, and the student's performance is closely monitored using a 'Picasso', which is, in fact, a colour code. The stress is a major hurdle for a lot of students, and the various CAP 10 checklists have been voluntarily extended in order to increase the student's workload in flight and on the ground to detect who can cope with the burden, and who cannot. Each year, about 24 students will make the grade and earn a short officer commission.

All Escadrille 50S flying instructors are active military servicemen drawn from the helicopter, fast jet and maritime patrol communities. Their extremely high level of qualification ensures a remarkable standard of flying, and the students benefit from a wealth of experience.

Proven CAP 10
The CAP 10 has proved ideal for screening and for elementary training. Its good performance and excellent agility, together with the perfect all-round visibility provided by its bubble canopy, are praised by both instructors and students. Additionally, its side-by-side seating is better adapted for elementary training than the tandem seating configuration of other trainers. The CAP 10 is a tail-dragger, so the instructors have to adhere to strict crosswind limits, which can prove to be a real challenge, especially in the winter when the grass runway at Lanvéoc-Poulmic is soaked with rain water. They are tasked to screen pilots, who will one day land on rolling and pitching aircraft carrier or frigate decks, probably the most difficult skill to master in the whole aviation world. They must be certain that the trainees have all the required qualities to learn rapidly how to operate a demanding aircraft. They make sure that the students quickly adapt to the CAP 10 and to the Navy way of flying, and they introduce them to all flight regimes and idiosyncrasies inherent in any aircraft. While teaching basic flying skills, they select the best students and prepare them for the next stages of their training syllabus. This is the reason why the CAP 10 proves ideal for the role. It is a difficult aircraft to land, especially in crosswinds, and instructors have no problem detecting which individuals cannot cope with the workload. Students having eyes/hands/feet co-ordination problems will also be easily detected in the CAP 10. Finally, only a few air clubs are equipped with CAP 10s, and, as a result, only a few students have flown the type before joining the Navy. A couple of years ago, all remaining CAP 10 trainers were upgraded to CAP 10C standard, with a carbon-fibre wing.

Different streams
Students who successfully pass the first hurdles follow a fighter lead-in module that comprises 11 sorties, five on the CAP 10C for formation flying and advanced aerobatics training and six on the SR20 for navigation training at 120 knots. The purpose of this short syllabus is to stream them according to their wishes and abilities. In the past, they were streamed at a later stage, but it was felt that a more cost-effective solution could be adopted. At the end of this module, students are assessed for fast jets, multi-engine or rotary streaming.

Below left: The French Navy is the last military operator of the classic Mudry CAP 10 trainer in France.

Below right: An Escadrille 50S CAP 10 taxies out at Lanvéoc-Poulmic for yet another sortie over the Crozon Peninsula, in Brittany.

Depending on available slots, future fast jet pilots follow one of two paths: they either go to Cognac to fly the Pilatus PC-21 with the Armée de l'Air et de l'Espace (AAE, or French Air and Space Force) or to Naval Air Station (NAS) Whiting Field to fly the T-6 Texan II with the US Navy. Later on, they will all move on to NAS Meridian for advanced tactical training on the T-45C Goshawk alongside their US Navy colleagues.

Future E-2C Hawkeye pilots also travel to the US for further training on the T-45 Goshawk at Meridian, and on the T-44 Pegasus (a military variant of the Beechcraft King Air) at NAS Corpus Christi.

Joint Rafale training squadron

At Saint-Dizier–Robinson Air Base, in Eastern France, future Rafale pilots undergo their conversion to type and conversion to role within Escadron de Transformation Rafale (ETR) 3/4 'Aquitaine', the AAE's dedicated Rafale operational conversion unit, part of the 4ème Escadre de Chasse (4th Fighter Wing). To carry out its mission, ETR 3/4 operates a mixed fleet of AAE Rafale B/C and Navy Rafale M fighters. Instructors are drawn from both the AAE and the Aéronautique Navale, the syllabus being the same for the young pilots of the two air arms. Students are trained to fly the Rafale and to operate it as a weapon system in both air-to-air and air-to-ground roles. They will first join the Aéronautique Navale conversion unit (Centre de Navalisation Rafale) at Landivisiau to learn specific naval skills, including carrier landings and anti-ship attack with Exocet missiles, before being sent to a frontline unit to complete their training and meet all the operational requirements.

On average, about half of French Navy students are sent directly to Landivisiau for a training course without going to Saint-Dizier. This typically happens when the ETR 3/4 'Aquitaine' is too busy training Air Force and foreign Rafale pilots, as was recently the case after Dassault Aviation won many export contracts.

Escadrille 50S flies a mixed fleet of CAP 10 and Cirrus SR20 trainers from Lanvéoc-Poulmic.

Multi-engine EMB121 Xingu

Trainee pilots selected for the multi-engine stream will follow a comprehensive syllabus, flying the Embraer EMB121 Xingu light transport aircraft of the Ecole de l'Aviation de Transport 00.319 (EAT 319), the AAE's transport aviation school located in Base Aérienne 702 Avord (Avord Air Base), near Bourges, in Central France.

Flottille 28F and its Xingus will be the next step for these pilots selected for the multi-engine stream. Future Atlantique 2, Gardian and Falcon 50 pilots will fly the Xingu from Lann-Bihoué for a couple of years, building up multi-engine experience as pilots and captains in command (including at low-level over the sea) before transferring to a maritime patrol or maritime surveillance squadron to fly the Atlantique 2, the Falcon 50 or the Gardian. On top of its training role, Flottille 28F also performs more traditional transport missions, including light spares delivery and VVIP transportation.

Dauphin N3 trainers in Brittany

Students selected for helicopters will join the French Army Aviation School after leaving Escadrille 50S. The Ecole de l'Aviation Légère de l'Armée de Terre (EALAT, French Army Light Aviation School) is in charge of the basic training of all French military helicopter pilots, including those of the AAE, the Armée de Terre (Land Force) and the Gendarmerie, plus those of the French Customs and Police. Future Navy helicopter pilots log 155 hours flying the EC120 NHE at Dax before moving on to an instrument flying rules (IFR) course, either at Le Luc, on the AS550 Fennec, or at Angoulème with Héli-Union, on the Dauphin N3. At this stage, the students come back to Lanvéoc-Poulmic for a 'navalisation' course on the Dauphin with Flottille 34F/ Ecole de Spécialisation sur Hélicoptères Embarqués (ESHE, or Embarked Helicopters Specialisation School). Until January 2021, the ESHE was part of Escadrille 22S, but that unit was renamed Flottille 34F to revive the former Lynx squadron number plate. Flottille 34F had temporarily disbanded in September 2020, when the Lynx was withdrawn from use after 42 years of sterling service.

In May 2018, the first of an initial batch of four AS365N3 Dauphin helicopters on loan from Belgian company NHV entered service with the French Navy at Lanvéoc-Poulmic. The NHV Dauphins are used to train pilots, winchmen and rescue divers. Although civilian-registered, they are operated in full military markings. They are flown by Flottille 34F military personnel, but their maintenance is performed by civilian NHV technicians. The contract presently held by NHV is due for renewal in 2023. Under the latest plans, the aircraft selected for that new, five-year contract should be replaced by the future H160M Guépard from 2028. It remains to be seen, however, whether the Guépard will be

Below left: **The student is normally seated on the left in the CAP 10. Parachutes are compulsory when flying the CAP 10.**

Below right: **Instructors usually spend one or two years screening and training young aircrews before being posted back to a front-line unit.**

Above: A student and an instructor prepare a sortie in one of Escadrille 50S's dedicated briefing rooms in Lanvéoc-Poulmic.

Left: The CAP 10 is still a sprightly performer! This aircraft performs a loop close to its Lanvéoc-Poulmic home base. The Escadrille 50S aircraft are often flown in weather that would keep civilian light aircraft pilots firmly on the ground.

Below: When the weather is good, the flying goes unabated. Here, SR20 and CAP 10 trainers are photographed between two sorties on Escadrille 50S flight line. The Cirrus SR20 fleet is flown by military personnel, owned by the private industry and maintained by contractors.

available on time and in sufficient numbers to replace the training aircraft or if the new contract will have to be extended by a year or two to give more time for the Guépard operational evaluation to be conducted before service entry.

Pilot training by the ESHE

The first full-scale course of five helicopter pilots graduated from the new Dauphin course on 17 January 2020 at Lanvéoc-Poulmic, a major event that confirmed that the fleet of leased Dauphin N3 rotorcraft was then fully up to speed. Flottille 34F's commanding officer, Lieutenant-Commander Gonnot, explained:

> Every year, we train 12 to 15 new pilots. We are currently increasing this flow to match the needs, as the Navy is moving ahead with plans to have two full crews for its Aquitaine-class multi-mission frigates. This means that we will double the number of NH90 Caïman detachments, but with the same number of aircraft. Each FREMM [Frégate Multi-Missions, multi-mission frigate] will have two helicopter detachments, and we have to progressively increase the number of pilots. Accordingly, the ESHE's allocation of flying hours has been boosted from 1,800 last year to 2,000 in 2021.

Right: Escadrille 50S is often called the 'Air Club' by other Aéronautique Navale units. Its instructors are all highly qualified.

Below: Being a tail-dragger, the CAP 10C proves challenging to land.

In September 2020, NHV added another Dauphin to the batch on loan to the French Navy, thus bringing the fleet to five aircraft. Lieutenant-Commander Gonnot continued:

> NHV is contractually bound to provide a minimum of three Dauphins, and up to four during the joint deck landing qualifications that are spread over two weeks to train Navy, Air Force, Army and Gendarmerie pilots. Providing four aircraft when you have only four in the inventory sometimes proves difficult, because you do not have any spare capacity when a mechanical problem occurs or when an aircraft has to undergo periodic maintenance. The arrival of the fifth Dauphin has given us added operational flexibility and increased capacity to absorb the workload.

A perfect type for the role

The replacement of the Alouette III with the Dauphin N3 in the training role is a major step forward. Lieutenant Pascal (surname withheld upon request), the officer in charge of the instruction within the ESHE, explained:

> The Alouette was a good training aircraft, but the Dauphin is clearly something else. The Dauphin is fitted with a state-of-the-art instrument panel with multifunction display, and with two turbines, like all helicopters in front line service. Another obvious advantage is that it is very similar to the other Dauphin variants and to the Panther in service with Flottille 35F and 36F. This means that the young pilots coming out of training will be totally operational on their new mount in a shorter amount of time, without a requirement for a conversion course. The aircraft is a twin, equipped with a three-axis autopilot, a radar and a night vision goggle (NVG)-compatible instrument panel. As a result, our students can now fly at night and work with ships in the dark, and even land at night on flight decks, and they are much better prepared to fly in realistic conditions, day and night. Its only drawback is that it is not fitted with a four-axis autopilot [pitch, roll, yaw and height above ground] that would have allowed us to teach winching at night above the water, simulating the rescue of a survivor.

The weather in Brittany can be a real problem for Escadrille 50S aircrews, especially in the winter.

Right: The French Navy is so pleased with its CAP 10s that two new-built CAP 10 NG trainers were recently ordered.

Below: The Armée de l'Air et de l'Espace (AEE, or French Air and Space Force) Pilatus PC-21 is now in service for advanced pilot training. About half of the future French Navy fighter pilots fly the PC-21 before switching to the T-45C Goshawk.

Rear crew training

French Navy helicopter tactical coordinators, winchmen/loadmasters and rescue divers all undergo specialised courses at bases Lanvéoc-Poulmic and Hyères. There is a lot of cross training between the two trades, as they will have to closely cooperate during an operational sortie. The winchmen/loadmasters are mainly trained to operate the winch and to use all the associated advanced winching techniques: over land winching, hoist malfunctions, over water winching, day and night deck winching, underslung load transport. As part of their training, all the divers attend an advanced medical course.

Fixed-winged rear crew training is performed on two AVDEF (Aviation Défense) Jetstream 41 twins flown from Lann-Bihoué. Tactical co-ordinators, radio operators, and radar operators/navigators learn how to operate their kit on these specially modified contractor-owned aircraft. For example, radar operators practise the basic manipulations of the radar: the effect of height, target aspect, weather, the radar homings, the different types of radar searches, of radar letdowns.

Future E-2C Hawkeye rear crew members all undergo a dedicated training course, focusing on fighter control techniques and tactics, learning how to position fighters in order to intercept a target and prevail in short-, medium- and long-range engagements. They are trained alongside the fighter controllers who will operate from dedicated anti-air ships like Forbin-class air-defence destroyers. This helps ensure full interoperability within the Navy, as everyone will be using common procedures.

About half of the trainees selected for the fighter stream will fly the T-6 Texan II with the US Navy before moving on to the T-45C Goshawk.

A Flottille 28F EMB 121 Xingu comes in to land at its Lann-Bihoué home base. The Xingu is used for multi-engine training by both the French Navy and the AAE.

Future Aéronautique Navale rotary pilots fly their first helicopter, the EC120 NHE, with the French Army at Dax.

Rotary instrument flying training is conducted at Le Luc on Army AS550 Fennec helicopters. The Fennec is the military variant of the acclaimed AS350 Squirrel.

Above: A Rafale B of Escadron de Transformation Rafale 3/4 (ETR 3/4) 'Aquitaine' photographed in Saint-Dizier. All future Navy and AAE Rafale pilots follow the same syllabus within the ETR.

Left: The replacement of the Alouette III by the Dauphin in the training role in 2018 was a huge step forward, as students can now fly a modern type fitted with the latest avionics.

Below: In order to safely operate over the sea, future helicopter pilots need to undergo a specific course, training how to land on ships, how to winch survivors out of a small pitching boat in all weathers and how to lift an underslung load from one vessel to another.

A Flottille 34F Dauphin N3 photographed during a winching exercise with training ship *Jules*. The small vessel was acquired specifically for the training role. The diver on the *Jules*' rear platform is preparing a foldable, hoistable stretcher.

Above: The Dauphin N3 is fitted with Electronic Flight Instrument System (EFIS) screens and offers more realistic training than the outdated Alouette III and its 'steam gauges'.

Right: Young naval aviators are all trained to very high standards.

A large percentage of the Dauphin training syllabus is flown in the simulator at Lanvéoc-Poulmic. Nowadays, female students are more present than ever.

CESSAN

All French Navy aircrews regularly attend courses at the Centre d'Entraînement au Sauvetage et à la Survie de l'Aéronautique Navale (CESSAN, or Naval Aviation Rescue and Survival Training Centre) for ab-initio survival training and refresher training. Prospective naval aircrews come to the CESSAN to learn the basic skills necessary to survive in the water in the event of a crash. This demanding course is spread over a week, and the candidates that do not make it through are eliminated from further aircrew training. Different types of exercises are performed in the state-of-the-art 40m (132ft) pool equipped with simulators and dunkers: for example, the students are dragged in the water and will have to get rid of their parachute harness. The modular dunkers that represent the cockpit of a Rafale strike fighter, a Tigre attack helicopter or the main cabin/cockpit of a NH90 Caïman are among the deepest going in the world (5m/16ft). The trainees have to learn the underwater egress techniques in all types of conditions, culminating in the night-time, upside-down scenario. Additionally, the students are given lectures on how to survive in different conditions, including in the arctic and in a desert. Finally, a small craft takes the airmen to sea, where they practise dinghy-boarding before being winched aboard a helicopter. Aéronavale aircrews have to come back periodically to check, during 'refresher' courses, that their survival techniques and knowledge are up to the desired standard. Furthermore, trainees from other branches of the French Armed Forces – Aviation Légère de l'Armée de Terre (ALAT, French Army Aviation), AAE, Gendarmerie and Direction générale de l'armement (DGA, the defence procurement agency) – regularly attend courses.

Above: VN *Partisan* is a privately operated ship that is under contract from the French Navy for a wide range of roles. It is notably used by Flottille 34F instructors to teach young pilots how to land on a ship.

Left: French Navy helicopter pilots are trained to fly in all sorts of weathers. Here, an Alouette III and a Dauphin fly in close formation in low clouds.

Once the Alouette III is withdrawn from use in late 2022, Flottille 34F will be entirely equipped with civilian-owned Dauphins.

One of the dunkers used by the Centre d'Entraînement au Sauvetage et à la Survie de l'Aéronautique Navale (CESSAN, Naval Aviation Rescue and Survival Training Centre) for egress training. This cabin is fully representative of that of a NH90 Caïman.

Above left: As all French Navy Rafales are single-seaters, instrument flying training needs to be done in another aircraft. This is where the Escadrille 57S Falcon 10s come in to play.

Left: An instructor helps a student during an indoor exercise within the CESSAN pool.

The Falcon 10 is capable of carrying up to seven VVIPs or light cargo in the transport role.

Above: The Ecole du Personnel de Pont d'Envol (EPPE, or Flight Deck Personnel School) handles the training of all future flight deck crews: aircraft handling and launch officers, plane directors, chains and chocks handlers, tractor drivers, helicopter control officers, enlisted landing signal specialists and cargo load spotters

Right: Future flight deck personnel and tractor drivers learn how to tow and chain down a Super Étendard fighter at the EPPE at Hyères.

Chapter 3
Carrier Aviation

Aircraft carrier *Charles de Gaulle* has been the French Navy flag ship for the last 20 years. Since entering service, the vessel and its carrier air group have been engaged in countless combat operations in Afghanistan, Libya and in Iraq and Syria against Daesh.

The *Charles de Gaulle* is a strategic combat tool that can be deployed anywhere in the world at short notice, covering more than 1,000km per day at 23kts. The French carrier air group has gained invaluable combat experience that has transformed the unit into a lethal and effective outfit.

Charles de Gaulle carrier

The 42,000-tonne *Charles de Gaulle* was conceived during the Cold War as a nuclear-powered strike carrier to replace the much smaller *Clemenceau* and *Foch*, both in service since the early 1960s. Compared with its predecessors, the new vessel was bigger and could carry heavier aircraft than the F-8 Crusader, Super Étendard, Étendard IV and Alizé then in service. The *Charles de Gaulle* is equipped with two US-built C13F catapults and three US-built arresting gears. It is fitted with extensive aviation maintenance facilities, including a reactor test bench where a Rafale's M88-2 turbofans can be pushed up to maximum power. Its carrier air group now typically comprises 24 Rafale fighters, two E-2C Hawkeye early warning aircraft, two Dauphin plane guard helicopters and one Caïman multirole helicopter. Should the need arise, the number of Rafales could surge to 30, bringing additional offensive and defensive capabilities.

The adoption of a very compact nuclear propulsion system enabled engineers to allocate bigger volumes to other functions, including aircraft maintenance and the storage of ammunition, food and spare parts. The need for marine fuel for ship propulsion disappeared too, allowing far more aviation fuel to be stored on board (4,000m³). Still, the *Charles de Gaulle* carries about 1,000 tonnes of diesel fuel for the safety engines that would be required to cool down the nuclear reactors should a problem occur. The vessel is also equipped with replenishment at sea gear that would allow it to refuel some of its escort with that diesel fuel, thus enhancing operational flexibility. Thanks to its two nuclear K15 reactors, the *Charles de Gaulle* can sustain its maximum speed of 27kts nearly indefinitely, and its escort sometimes has difficulty keeping pace as diesel/turbine-powered frigates guzzle fuel at an alarming rate at such a high speed. This is the reason why the carrier's replenishment at sea capability proves so important, giving the task force commander the option of toping up the tanks of the escort vessels.

Remarkably stable platform

The French Navy's stringent requirements for sea keeping qualities led to the development of innovative stabilisation systems that enable the movement in roll to be countered: the ship can turn hard to port or starboard without tilting right or left, with the flight deck remaining horizontal for safety reasons. This was achieved using weights that move athwartship on rails to help counter the roll, and stabilising ailerons on each side, port and starboard, below the waterline. Thanks to gyroscopic information, the ailerons are hydraulically activated to stabilise the ship in roll in a strong sea swell.

Since entering service, the vessel has proved incredibly reliable and dependable, spending more days at sea per annum, on average, than any other carrier in the world. In 2018, it underwent a comprehensive mid-life upgrade that will enable it to remain in service until 2038–40. That upgrade was extensive. The two nuclear reactors were refilled, and countless systems were replaced or overhauled. Its French-built landing mirror gave way to a US-sourced IFLOLS (Improved Fresnel Lens Optical Landing System). The vessel's combat information centre was completely reworked, with the old workstations being replaced by commercially available off-the-shelf screens and keyboards. These screens are directly fed by the latest generation of calculators powered by an advanced software, giving operators a perfect understanding of the evolving tactical situation around the task force. Two cyber defence centres were created on board the carrier to handle cyber threats. For battle damage resilience, they are widely separated within the ship. The carrier's sensor suite was upgraded too, with the replacement of the outdated DRBJ-11B radar by a more recent Thales Smart-S radar, which offers significantly improved detection and tracking performance. All systems are now connected through a fibre-optics network.

Rafale M omnirole fighter

The French Navy became the first operator of the Rafale anywhere when the first two aircraft were delivered to Landivisiau Naval Air Base, Brittany, in late 2000. Today, three naval squadrons, Flottilles 11F, 12F and 17F, all stationed at Landivisiau, operate the Rafale Marine fighter. They form the spearhead of the French Navy offensive force.

Right from the start of the programme, the Rafale was designed for carrier operations. Its canard foreplanes/delta wing configuration offers an excellent compromise between agility in combat,

The *Charles de Gaulle* at sea, off its Toulon homeport, in late 2018. The vessel had just come out of its mid-life upgrade. The massive island accommodates the task force command post.

radius of action, payload and handling qualities in the aircraft carrier circuit. Compared to the AAE variant, the Rafale Marine is fitted with an internal electrically deploying/folding ladder, helping reduce the amount of equipment required on deck. Its airframe is easy to maintain at sea, with corrosion resistance taken into account during the design phase. To reduce costs and ease spares inventory management, the Rafale Marine retains an extremely high level of commonality with its AAE cousins.

The carrier launch procedure is highly automated, as the Rafale is fitted with a dedicated catapulting mode that handles everything, automatically controlling the launch and climb-out for the first 10 to 15 seconds of the flight. When the catapult fires, the pilot does not need to use the side-stick controller: as soon as it leaves the catapult and clears the deck, the fighter adopts the desired nose-high climbing attitude until reaching 300ft above sea level. Between 300ft and 400ft, the pilot progressively regains control. Even with full forward stick, the aircraft would keep on climbing, and the M88 turbofans are so powerful that, even if one fails on take-off, the fighter can safely fly out (even though external loads might have to be punched out in heavy configurations).

In the carrier circuit, the Rafale is rock-steady, proving extremely stable in all conditions. Its airframe was optimised for a low approach speed and its M88-2 engines are both powerful and very responsive, a crucial advantage 'in the groove', during the final approach prior to landing, when power needs to be constantly adjusted to remain on a perfect glide path. Its advanced autothrottle system is much more sophisticated than a traditional autothrottle: it is coupled with both the engines and the airframe's control surfaces, which can be automatically deflected for maximum braking effect. This so-called 'thrust/drag control mode' enables the aircraft to automatically keep a chosen Mach number (above 20,000ft), an indicated air speed (below 20,000ft) or an angle of attack number (when the undercarriage is down) in an extremely wide flying envelope. For example, for a clean Rafale with its gear down, the autothrottle automatically keeps a 16-degree angle of attack (AOA) and a 124kt approach speed.

Eight Rafales and one Dauphin on the *Charles de Gaulle*'s flight deck during carrier qualifications. A wave of four Rafales will soon be launched.

Right: Four Rafales parked on the *Charles de Gaulle* flight deck, behind the massive island.

Below: Carrier *Charles de Gaulle* can carry up to 600 tonnes of ammunition. Here, an assortment of precision weapons is on display. From front to rear: GBU-49 Enhanced Paveway, GBU-58 Paveway II, AASM Hammer™ and GBU-12 Paveway II.

Incremental approach

From the start of its design process, the Rafale was developed to incorporate new weapons, sensors and systems continuously and easily. Rafales were delivered to the French Navy in five main successive standards that each offered incremental operational capabilities:

- Inducted in 2000, the initial Standard F1 specialised in the air-to-air role with its radar-guided Mica RF missiles, its infrared-guided Magic 2 missiles and its 30M791 30mm internal cannon fed with 125 rounds. It was also equipped with the buddy-buddy in-flight refuelling pod.
- Appearing in 2006, the Standard F2 brought initial air-to-ground capabilities, thanks to the adoption of the GBU-12 Paveway II laser-guided bombs, the AASM Hammer™ (Armement Air-Sol Modulaire Highly Agile and Manoeuvrable Munition Extended Range) family of precision weapons and the Scalp stealth cruise missile. Air-to-air capabilities were significantly expanded with the introduction of the infrared-guided Mica IR, which was considerably more capable than the Magic 2, the L16 datalink to automatically share data with allied assets and the Front Sector Optronics (FSO) system to passively track and identify hostile aircraft at stand-off distances.
- Entering service in 2008, the Standard F3 was the first to offer full operational capabilities. It was equipped with the ASMP-A (Air-Sol Moyenne Portée Amélioré, improved medium range air-to-surface) nuclear-tipped ramjet-propelled missile, the AM39 Exocet anti-ship missile, the GBU-24 Paveway III laser-guided bomb, the Damoclès targeting pod, and the Pod Reco NG (new generation recce pod).
- Introduced in the French Navy in 2013, Standard F3O4T focused on various avionics improvements, including the arrival of the Active Electronically Scanned Array (AESA) technology for the RBE2 radar, of the FSO-IT (Improved Technologies) and of the Détecteur de Départ Missile de Nouvelle Génération (DDM-NG, or new generation missile launch detector).
- At the time of writing, the Standard F3R was the latest software drop in service. This new evolution is cleared to carry the TALIOS (TArgeting Long-Range Identification Optronic System) new generation targeting pod and to fire the Meteor ramjet-powered air-to-air missile and the GBU-16 Paveway II laser-guided bomb. It is also equipped with a new generation in-flight refuelling pod.

Two Rafales simulate a dogfight. Even in a very heavy configuration with four drop tanks, a refuelling pod and two Mica missiles like the aircraft in the foreground, the Rafale remains remarkably agile.

Looking further ahead, the development of the Rafale F4 was launched in 2019, and flight trials of the first system began in 2021. Service entry will occur from 2024 in different blocks, which will bring new systems and incremental capabilities, including new, larger, touchscreen digital lateral displays; improvements to the Spectra self-defence/electronic warfare suite; a modern Infrared Search and Track (IRST) system for the Rafale's FSO, Ground Moving Target Indicator (GMTI) and Synthetic Aperture Radar modes for the electronic scanning radar; a new carrier landing aid to decrease pilot workload and reduce short/long dispersion when catching the wire; a communication server to manage all internal and external data exchange; a helmet-mounted display; and a new intra-flight datalink. The 1,000kg variant of Hammer and the Mica NG (new generation) air-to-air will also be adopted for the F4 standard.

Inherently multirole

All Rafale Flottilles are cleared to perform the whole range of combat missions: nuclear deterrence, fleet air-defence, escort, sweep, pre-strategic and tactical reconnaissance, destruction of enemy air-defences, anti-ship strikes, deep precision strikes, air interdiction, close air support, and buddy-buddy refuelling. Captain Marc (surname withheld upon request), a fighter specialist with the Aéronautique Navale Command, explains:

> The huge advantage of the Rafale is its inherent operational flexibility and its ability to plug into French and allied command and control networks to share tactical data. With the Rafale, you have that 'Day One' entry capability that allows you to carry out your mission and attack targets, even in contested environments, against an enemy equipped with the latest air-defence systems. With its assortment of Meteor and Mica air-to-air missiles, the Rafale can fight its way in to deliver a military effect. The fighter can be armed with a whole array of long-range weapons, including Scalp cruise missiles, to destroy high-value targets at stand-off distances.

Two Rafales demonstrating their buddy-buddy in-flight refuelling capabilities. All Navy Rafales are single-seaters.

A small cadre of Rafale pilots are qualified to operate the ASMP-A nuclear missile as part of the French nuclear deterrence policy. They undergo a strict selection process and a rigorous training programme. The highly secretive ramjet-propelled missile can be used against land targets or naval forces at sea.

To hone their skills, Rafale pilots regularly participate in international exercises, such as Joint Warrior, off Scotland, or the Tactical Leadership Programme, in Albacete, Spain. French Rafales frequently train with US Navy fighters and regularly operate from US aircraft carriers, thus demonstrating total interoperability with their American counterparts. They also routinely train with, and against contractor-operated jets, such as the Aermacchi MB-339 trainers flown by French company Ares to provide basic training at reduced costs.

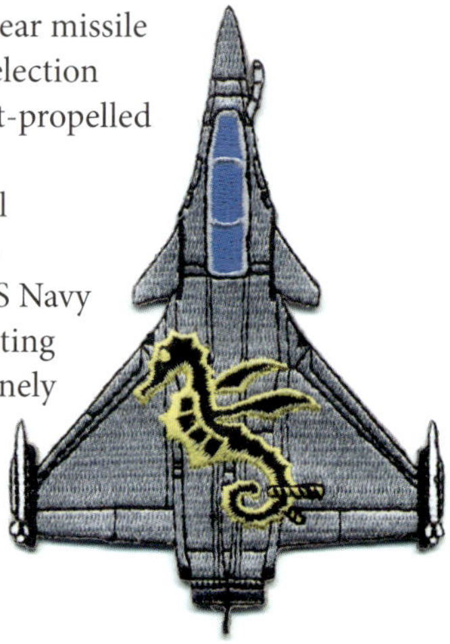

The E-2C Hawkeye

Three E-2C Hawkeye early warning aircraft are in service with Flottille 4F based at Lann-Bihoué, Brittany. The aircraft were delivered to Lann-Bihoué in 1998, 1999 and 2003 in a hybrid standard, a kind of mix between the Group II Nav Upgrade and the Hawkeye 2000, the latest standard at the time. From the Group II Nav Upgrade, they got the APS-145 radar, the workstation, the main computer, a GPS and the ALR-73 electronic intelligence (ELINT) system. From the improved Hawkeye 2000, they received the vapour cycle cooling system and more powerful electric generators.

Since entering service, the French Hawkeyes have been regularly updated at the Cuers depot, in the south of France, to provide progressively expanded operational capabilities and to keep them

A pair of Rafales photographed off Brittany in a playful mood. Even with two drop tanks, the Rafale is incredibly nimble.

operationally relevant. The adoption of a new central mission computer, the Tactical Computer Group (TCG), was one of the most significant upgrades French Hawkeyes ever went through. The TCG is much more reliable and stable than the previous one they had. The second most important modification was the introduction of the new NP2000 Kevlar eight-bladed propellers that proved more reliable. In 2003, the first Hawkeye was modified to accommodate a Satcom (Satellite communications) radio, and the other two aircraft were subsequently similarly modified.

If needed, French technicians can autonomously support and modify the Hawkeye for very specific needs. For drug-interdiction missions in 2008, French Hawkeyes were fitted with the Automatic Identification System (AIS) used to precisely locate and identify shipping at sea or at anchor. The AIS was adapted to the Hawkeye by French engineers, all the work being done internally in less than two months. A touchscreen was also installed in the cockpit. Called MARC DL, for Multi-Asset Recording Computer for Data Links, it allows the captain and the co-pilot to have direct access to the tactical situation and to all L16 data.

Eye in the sky

The Hawkeye has proved to be an invaluable asset, providing 360-degree coverage against air and surface contacts to increase the task force's situational awareness. Initially envisioned as a purely airborne early warning asset, the aircraft has progressively become a flying command and control centre, a communication relay and a flying datalink node.

Flown by a crew of two pilots and three weapon system operators, the E-2C is utilised by the French Navy for an extremely wide range of missions, including sea and air surveillance around the task force. They control fighters when they go 'feet dry' to attack targets on the ground, helping coordinate overland missions and ensuring deconfliction between friendlies, during the ingress and egress. Once in their operating area, they become an 'Airborne Battlefield Command and Control Centre' in charge of the tactical coordination. They very rapidly connect people, fighters and tankers, for instance, or forward air controllers and fire support aircraft, be they fighters or helicopters. During an amphibious operation, Flottille 4F would be in charge of providing early detection of airborne and surface threats and of guiding the interceptors that would protect the vulnerable amphibious ships.

The Dassault Aviation Rafale is powered by two M88-2 engines, each rated at 75kN (17,000lb).

Thanks to their Quick Draw interrogator designed to 'talk' to the PRC-112G two-way transceiver allocated to each fighter pilot, Flottille 4F Hawkeyes are fully capable of participating in combat search and rescue (CSAR) missions to help recover a pilot stranded behind enemy lines. Flottille 4F is also capable of supporting various law enforcement missions at sea, from maritime counter-terrorism actions to drug interdiction, and from SAR coordination to anti-piracy surveillance.

With its sensors in the nose and tail, and with its large conformal antenna that runs along the right-hand side of the fuselage, the Hawkeye has long been well equipped for the crucial ELINT mission. The French Hawkeyes have now received the ALQ-217 ELINT system, which offers considerably expanded operational capabilities, thus supplanting the ALR-73 that had proved more and more difficult to support.

Towards the E-2D Advanced Hawkeye

In late 2020, it was officially announced by the Ministry of the Armed Forces that three E-2D Advanced Hawkeyes were to be ordered to replace the current E-2Cs. Compared to their ageing predecessors, they will bring even more impressive detection capabilities to the French carrier task force. With their combined AESA/mechanical-scanning APY-9 radar, they will be able to detect and track the latest threats, including stealth cruise missiles and small unmanned aerial vehicles (UAVs), at extended ranges in difficult conditions. The French Navy is in no hurry to receive its E-2Ds, however, as its E-2Cs are meticulously maintained and regularly updated. This means that, according to the latest plans, the French aircraft will be the last E-2D Advanced Hawkeyes to come out of the Northrop Grumman production line, unless other customers are found or the production run for the US Navy is extended.

The Rafale has been designed to perform the whole spectrum of air-to-air and air-to-surface missions. Dassault Aviation uses the word 'omnirole' to describe the capabilities of its Rafale fighter, meaning it can undertake the whole range of nuclear and conventional combat missions from land bases or aircraft carriers.

Carrier rotary assets

The *Charles de Gaulle* now sails with a single Flottille 31F Caïman and two Flottille 35F Dauphin Pedro helicopters. To provide CSAR cover to fast jet aircrews, AAE EC725 Caracals of Escadron d'Hélicoptères 1/67 'Pyrénées' will deploy on board *Charles de Gaulle*.

The SA365F Dauphins' main role is to provide plane guard duties, standing ready to rescue, day and night, any Rafale pilot or Hawkeye crew that would have had to eject or ditch after a technical problem. The Dauphins are well equipped for the role, and they systematically carry a specialist rescue diver for each plane guard mission. They also stand ready to perform more traditional SAR missions. If needed, they can be armed with a door-mounted 7.62mm machine gun to enhance force protection, when crossing a strait for example, or to provide fire support during board, visit, search and seize operations. They are also tasked with transport missions for personnel and small cargo and sometimes perform vertical replenishment at sea with an underslung load.

The French Navy took advantage of the withdrawal of the Super Étendard and of the switch to an 'all Rafale' naval fighter wing to radically modify the role of the Pedro helicopter. Lieutenant-Commander Féraud explained:

> A risk assessment study was carried out after the switch to a fighter fleet entirely composed of twin-engine fighters, and we came to the conclusion that the risk of an ejection had seriously receded. In turn, this led to major changes for the Pedro detachment, with the appearance of a new operational doctrine, more oriented towards the tactical role, as for the US Navy's MH-60S Seahawk fleet. Until 2018, Pedro helicopters only performed occasional ship-to-shore logistics sorties and flew rigid patterns during fast jet carrier ops, on the port side of the carrier in day light and on the starboard side at night. The range of roles performed by Pedro aircrews has significantly been expanded to include maritime surveillance ahead of the task force, force protection, commandos support and logistics and light transport. Our Dauphin Pedros now fly 50 nautical miles away from the carrier while remaining available to rescue an ejectee. Mission profile is adapted to the circumstances, however: for example, during a carrier qualification campaign when young fighter pilots log their first carrier traps, the Pedro will remain close to the *Charles de Gaulle*.

A fully armed Rafale, photographed from a C-135FR Stratotanker. It is equipped with two Mica air-to-air missiles, four AASM Hammer stand-off precision weapons, one Damoclès targeting pod and two 2,000-litre drop tanks.

To meet the requirement for tactically oriented missions, the three Dauphin Pedro helicopters have recently been upgraded with an NVG-compatible instrument panel. Like the Panthers of Flottille 36F, the three aircraft will shortly receive a Mode 5 IFF.

Caïman multirole chopper

The NH90 Caïman is the latest addition to the carrier air group, the type having recently replaced the single Alouette III that had been carried since the *Charles de Gaulle*'s entry into service. Compared to the totally outdated Alouette III, the Caïman offers massively expanded operational capabilities, albeit at the cost of a much larger footprint on board the carrier. Its main role is to perform surface surveillance/targeting missions and to provide logistics support to the task force. In the 1980s and 1990s, the logistics mission was carried out by Super Frelons, but that role had progressively been taken over by French Army Puma helicopters specially detached on board *Charles de Gaulle*. The NH90 is large enough to carry internally a M88-2 turbofan. It can also lift a hefty load and can be used for vertical replenishment. Like the Dauphin, it can be armed with a door-mounted 7.62mm machine gun for fire support and force protection. With its powerful ENR (European Naval Radar) and its Forward Looking Infrared (FLIR) turret, it is fully capable of undertaking maritime surveillance missions ahead of the naval force. The NH90 can also be used in support of special operations, closely cooperating with French Navy commandos that are often part of the task force. If needed, in times of crisis or war, it could also be fitted with sonar and torpedoes to reinforce the anti-submarine capabilities of the carrier strike group. In an emergency, the NH90 could also undertake combat recoveries when Caracals are not on board.

A Mototok electric tractor pushes back a Rafale in the *Charles de Gaulle*'s **hangar.**

The *Charles de Gaulle* main hangar can be divided into two different bays to boost resilience against fires and battle damage.

Above: The *Charles de Gaulle* is equipped to perform in-depth aircraft maintenance. The vessel carries a huge spares inventory and has large maintenance facilities.

Right: The French carrier is fitted with an engine maintenance shop and an engine test bay where Rafale M88-2 turbofans can be checked up to maximum afterburner power.

Above: This Rafale has just caught the wire during a night carrier landing exercise at Landivisiau.

Left: A Rafale in one of the Flottille 12F hangars at Landivisiau. The red lighting is a Navy way of telling this is nighttime.

Below: Rafales prepared for flight at Landivisiau. Night training is routinely conducted by French Navy pilots.

Within the next few seconds, Rafale M42 will be catapulted away for a night training mission.

Above left: A fully armed Rafale taxies out on the *Charles de Gaulle*. It is fitted with four GBU-12 laser-guided bombs, two 2,000-litre drop tanks, and two Mica air-to-air missiles.

Above right: The AASM Hammer precision weapon is rocket-boosted for greater range and higher impact energy.

Below: In a few seconds, this Rafale will blast away from the catapult on its way towards a target in Libya in 2011. The Rafale is the ideal combat tool for 'Day One' theatre entry, even against the latest threats.

A clean Rafale manoeuvres at high level. The fighter's advanced aerodynamic design provides a high level of agility.

Above: The Rafale is a combat proven and fully mature fighter that is regularly updated.

Below: French Navy Flottille 4F, callsign Damo, operates three E-2C Hawkeye early warning aircraft from its Lann-Bihoué home base and from the deck of the *Charles de Gaulle* carrier.

Above: The first Hawkeye arrived at Lann-Bihoué in December 1998, followed by the second one in April 1999. The option for a third Hawkeye was firmed up in November 1998, with delivery in 2003. The order for a fourth aircraft never materialised.

Left: With the E-2C Hawkeye, the Standard F3R Rafale, the *Charles de Gaulle* carrier and the new, state-of-the-art anti-air-warfare destroyers and frigates, the French Navy fields a coherent and modern air-defence and power-projection force.

The antenna of the Hawkeye's Satcom system is located atop the rotodome in an effort to obtain the best angular coverage.

Above: The Hawkeye has become a crucial asset and has become the 'Swiss Army knife' of the French carrier air wing. For the task force commander, the multirole Hawkeye is a powerful command and control tool capable of keeping a watchful eye on all hostile maritime and airborne activity around the fleet.

Right: French Hawkeyes play an increasing role in sea surveillance, guiding Rafale fighters to identify all shipping at up to ten or 12 sailing hours ahead of the fleet when transiting through dangerous waters, such as straits, which leaves ample time for the commander to make a tactical decision if the need arises after a threat is detected.

The Hawkeye's ability to plug into multinational communication networks is also a key parameter that has helped the French Navy reach new levels of operational credibility in the eyes of its closest allies.

A Flottille 4F E-2C Hawkeye stowed away for the night in the *Charles de Gaulle*'s cavernous hangar.

Above: The right engine of this Hawkeye has just been started. The whole procedure is closely monitored by Flottille 4F engineers.

Below: The Hawkeye is an extremely powerful aircraft that offers an impressive climb rate, a major advantage when being catapulted away from an aircraft carrier.

This Hawkeye taxies towards the lateral catapult. In the background, a SA365F Dauphin Pedro will soon fly away to provide SAR coverage.

Right: Flottille 35F relinquished its last Alouette III in 2019, leaving the Dauphin Pedro as the main French Navy plane guard duty asset.

Below: Three Dauphin Pedro helicopters are in the inventory, with two in service with the unit at any given time while the third is either in short term storage or undergoing deep maintenance.

AAE EC725 Caracals operate from the *Charles de Gaulle* to provide combat search and rescue (CSAR) coverage to the carrier air group.

Compared to the Alouette III, the Dauphin Pedro offers expanded capabilities and can perform missions day and night while the Alouette was restricted to daylight missions only.

An Escadrille 57S Falcon 10 comes in to land at Landivisiau. Escadrille 57S handles all fast jet pilots' instrument flying training.

Above: The avionics suites of all six Falcon 10s in French Navy inventory were extensively modernised in the mid-2010s, helping ensure the aircraft remains fully compliant with the latest regulations.

Below: All French Navy fighter pilots undertake instrument flying initial and continuation training on the Falcon 10MER (Marine Entraînement Radar, or naval radar training) of Escadrille 57S based at Landivisiau.

Chapter 4
Navy Helicopters at Sea

A wide array of French Navy surface combatants, surveillance vessels, trial ships and support vessels carry Panther, Caïman, Dauphin and Alouette III helicopters.

The Dauphin/Panther family and the NH90 Caïman have become the French Navy's main rotorcraft types, performing a wide range of missions ashore and at sea while the days of the Alouette III are counted.

Flottille 36F Panthers
Sixteen AS565SA Panthers (15 ordered by the Navy and one further aircraft transferred from the French flight test centre) have been delivered to the French Navy. Flown by Flottille 36F, out of Hyères, they perform a wide variety of roles, including maritime surveillance, intelligence, surveillance and reconnaissance (ISR), target designation for the MM40 Exocet missiles carried by their mother ships and for fighter strikes, naval gunfire terminal control, illegal traffic interdiction, maritime counter-terrorism, counter-piracy, SAR, force protection/fire support with a pintle-mounted 7.62mm machine-gun, cargo and passenger transport.

In French Navy service, the Panther has proved remarkably reliable, dependable and affordable. Although derived from a purely civilian rotorcraft, its airframe is well adapted to operations at sea, and the type is easy to maintain and repair, with spares widely available. Panthers routinely operate with French Navy commandos, including sniper teams, in the traffic interdiction role. They play an active role in hunting drug traffickers from surveillance frigates based in the French islands in the Caribbean. Their scoreboard is quite impressive as, over the course of the last few years, aircrews have helped keep dozens of tonnes of drugs, worth hundreds of millions of dollars, off the street. The Panther proves so quiet that drug dealers often do not realise they are there until it is already too late for them. The French Navy snipers flying with Flottille 36F are remarkably proficient and can deliver devastatingly accurate fires with their powerful 12.7mm (0.50in) rifles: a single shot is usually enough to stop a go-fast.

Standard 2
From 2010, the Panthers were all brought up to Standard 2. The upgraded programme included the adoption of a Euroflir™ 410 EO gyrostabilised turret mounted on the left side of the fuselage, the same as the one of the NH90, but with an even better man-machine interface, a laser rangefinder and a new daylight optical camera. Its performance levels are clearly outstanding, and Panther aircrews can now identify their prey at standoff distances, day and night. In the rear cabin, a new console has been fitted for the sensor operator. The beauty of the system is that the operator in the back has direct access to an enormous amount of data, including the AIS database and the French Navy shipping database, which includes thousands of photos of civilian and military ships. They can compare the actual FLIR image with a stored reference to positively identify a contact.

For increased interoperability with other French and NATO assets, the Standard 2 Panther is fitted with the L11 datalink, which has replaced the Titus system that relied on the slow and outdated L14, first introduced on the Alizé carrier-borne maritime patrol aircraft. At the time of writing, the French Navy was looking at various options to replace the Panther's semi-panoramic ORB32 radar, an ageing system.

New glass cockpit

The Panther's instrument panel has been upgraded from analogue instruments to glass-cockpit standard with Electronic Flight Instrument System (EFIS) screens. Each pilot now has a primary flight display and a navigation display at their disposal. The mission commander on the left also has the unchanged radar display and the new FLIR display. The navigation suite has been extensively modernised, and the Nadir Doppler and the stand-alone GPS gave way to a GPS-hybridised CMA-9000 calculator, which offers a wide range of operating modes, including civilian IFR modes and military-type search patterns used for SAR and operational missions. The adoption of the CMA-9000 has radically changed the way pilots operate, as they now have at their disposal a permanent database with the approach maps for all the airfields in France, Europe and even the whole world. Any of these maps can be called on the navigation display as required.

All the navigation and communication systems (one HF and two V/UHF radios with encryption and frequency agility capabilities, one VOR/ILS receiver, one TACAN, one ADF and two GPS receivers) are now controlled via a single, user-friendly electronic display unit. The Marine VHF is still a stand-alone radio, however. Since entering service, the Panther has proved to be an incredibly successful and flexible combat platform, performing countless missions in often difficult conditions. With the Standard 2, Flottille 36F is equipped with a very efficient maritime surveillance and combat tool.

Heavy rotary-wing asset

Flottille 31F, at Hyères, and Flottille 33F, in Lanvéoc-Poulmic, operate the NH90 Caïman Marine, the French Navy's heavy multirole helicopter. A total of 27 NH90s have been ordered for the Aéronautique Navale, split into 14 of the NHC (C for Combat) variant to supplant the Lynx, and 13 of the ramp-equipped NHS (S for Soutien, or Support) version to replace the Super Frelon. In fact, both variants can be equipped with a sonar kit to carry out anti-submarine warfare (ASW) missions, and any aircraft can be flown for any mission, even though a ramp equipped Caïman is usually allocated to the *Charles de Gaulle* detachment for logistics missions.

The first Caïman was delivered to the Aéronavale on 5 May 2010 for operational evaluation by the Centre d'Expérimentations Pratiques et de Réception de l'Aéronautique Navale/Escadrille 10S (CEPA/10S, the French Navy operational evaluation centre). At the time of writing, 26 Caïmans had

Below left: A Flottille 36F AS565SA Panther breaks away from the camera-ship. The Panther is a military variant of the Dauphin.

Below right: This Flottille 36F Panther manoeuvres at low-level over the sea.

been delivered to the French Navy, with the final one expected shortly. The NH90's entry into service has proved to be rather difficult, with aircraft being delivered in too many different sub-standards and configurations. The situation is slowly improving, however, as early aircraft are brought up to more recent standards, thus improving commonality in order to simplify support procedures.

ASW specialist

Equipped with a FLASH (Folding Light Acoustic System for Helicopters) dunking sonar, sonobuoys and MU90 torpedoes, the Caïman is the French Navy's main embarked ASW aircraft. Operating from the Aquitaine-class multi-mission stealth frigates, the Caïman can protect a task force at sea and engage hostile submarines that would threaten the naval force. The FLASH sonar has proved very popular and has been selected, among a wide number of customers, by the Royal Navy for the AgustaWestland Merlin HM1 and HM2 variants of the AW101, and by the US Navy for the

Above: Like its Dauphin civilian counterpart, the Panther is an attractive looking helicopter, with beautiful and sleek lines.

Below left: Standard 2 Panthers are equipped with the Euroflir™ 410, an EO gyrostabilised turret that has proved highly successful in French service.

Below right: This head-on shot shows the Panther's massive rescue hoist and its Euroflir 410 FLIR turret.

MH-60R (as the AQS-22 Airborne Low Frequency Sonar built under licence by Raytheon). The lightweight FLASH offers extended detection ranges. With its very long winch cable, it can be lowered very deep to track targets hidden below the thermocline layer, considerably improving the naval force's situational awareness. The FLASH is able to operate in various modes, including continuous wave for Doppler detection and measurement, and frequency modulation with signal compression/processing for increased resolution at long ranges. Although aircrews cannot disclose classified data, they can, nevertheless, reveal that the FLASH's detection range is more than five times better than that of the Lynx's DUAV-4 sonar. Various types of active and passive sonobuoys can also be carried by French NFH90s in an integrated dispenser to supplement the sonar and help improve ASW coverage in a given area.

MU90 torpedo

For ASW, the NH90 can carry two MU90 Impact torpedoes or two 300-litre external fuel tanks (or one of each for added endurance). The MU90 is a new generation torpedo that has been selected for a wide array of platforms by Australia, Denmark, France, Germany, Italy and Poland. Jointly developed by France and Italy, the 324mm MU90 is fitted with a powerful shaped charge warhead optimised to penetrate the latest and thickest submarine pressure hulls, and its acoustic active/passive sensor can defeat the latest known countermeasures and decoys. According to data provided by a Eurotorp brochure, the MU90's speed can vary from 29 to 50 knots, and the 314.1kg weapon boasts a range of 12,000m (13,123 yards) at full speed, and up to 25,000m (27,340 yards) at minimum velocity. It can engage surface targets and submarines at depths ranging from 3m only down to more than 1,000m. The weapon can be accurately programmed before firing. Depending on the sea state, the desired search pattern, the selected initial torpedo depth, and the requested firing mode, pre-set data is transferred from the NH90 to the MU90 via an advanced control unit.

Anti-surface warfare asset

With its ENR radar, its nose-mounted Euroflir 410 electro-optical detection/surveillance/tracking turret and its L11 datalink, the Caïman is ideally equipped to perform anti-surface warfare (ASuW) missions from a destroyer or a frigate. These missions include force protection, interceptions of pirates' skiffs or go-fasts used by drug traffickers, target designation for raids of Rafale naval strike fighters and beyond-the-horizon targeting for MM40 Exocet missiles launched by a surface ship.

The Panther is a multirole platform capable of undertaking a wide range of missions. Flottille 36F has forged strong bonds with the special forces community during narcotics operations and special operations.

Mounted in a fairing below the forward fuselage, the ENR (European Naval Radar) pulse-compression multimode radar provides 360 degrees of coverage, with full frequency agility for increased resistance to jamming. The ENR is optimised for the long-range detection of surface targets in difficult conditions, and can localise small echoes, such as periscopes, in high sea states. The gyrostabilised Euroflir system is used for target identification and designation at stand-off ranges, day or night. The L11 helps aircrews build up an unambiguous tactical picture around the fleet and share data with other naval and airborne assets, but it is increasingly outdated, and the NH90 will be among the platforms to be equipped with the future Link 22. For increased survivability against hostile surface combatants and interceptors, the helicopter is fitted with a comprehensive self-defence suite, which comprises a radar warning receiver, a missile approach warner and Saphir flare and chaff dispensers.

The Caïman has become the platform of choice for the maritime counter-terrorism role. It can be fitted with a modular mount that provides added stability when PGM, McMillan or Barrett 0.5in (12.7mm) high-power precision rifles are used by Commandos de Marine snipers in the maritime counter-terrorism role or for drug trafficking interdiction. It is also fully compatible with the MAG 58 7.62mm machine gun.

Crew of three

Like the AW101 Merlin, the NFH90 was optimised from the outset to be operated by a crew of three: pilot, 'Tacco' (tactical coordinator) and 'Senso' (sensor operator). Generally speaking, the Tacco would be the mission commander but the pilot, as the rotorcraft captain, has the right to veto their decisions. Both of them sit in the front cockpit, behind a state-of-the-art instrument panel composed of five multifunction displays: two for flight information and aircraft systems (hydraulics, electrics, fuel) and three for mission/tactical data, including radar and FLIR pictures. In the back, the Senso sits in front of a removable workstation fitted with three multifunction screens. Another workstation can be installed for an instructor or for a second Senso for very complex missions. It would then be utilised to significantly increase the number of sonobuoys that could be monitored simultaneously, and to boost the capabilities of the helicopter in the field of electronic warfare in a dense electromagnetic environment.

On the Caïman, the Tacco plays a pivotal role: they process the vast amount of data generated by the various on-board and off-board sensors, select the most useful information, determine the priorities and communicate with the naval force.

Below left: Flottille 36F helicopters spend most of their time flying low above the sea.

Below right: The Panther will eventually be replaced by the future H160M Guépard helicopter, a much bigger type.

Panthers are not fitted with a dunking sonar and cannot perform anti-submarine missions.

Classic Alouette III

The Alouette III is now a fast-disappearing breed. The faithful light helicopter has served the French Navy well, but the type is fast ageing, with maintenance becoming a problem, and Dauphins are progressively replacing the type. Eight SA319 Alouette IIIs are still allocated to Flottille 34F, including two in the Pacific, which deploy on board surveillance frigates *Vendémiaire*, at Nouméa, New Caledonia, and *Prairial*, at Papeete, Tahiti.

Within Flottille 34F/ESHE, the French Navy operates two permanent detachments that can deploy to a variety of vessels (trial ship *Monge*, frigate *Latouche-Tréville*, amphibious warfare ships *Mistral*, *Tonnerre* and *Dixmude* or any of the three remaining fleet replenishers) depending on operational requirements. The nimble Alouette III carries out a wide range of missions at sea. One of two detachment commanders, Lieutenant Nicolas explained:

The Alouette is a truly multirole platform. We are tasked to carry personnel between the ship and the shore, to lift equipment and stores during replenishments at sea, to perform maritime surveillance around our mother ship, and to launch for search and rescue, but in daylight only. In March 2021, during a deployment on board *Dixmude*, we participated in an important counter-narcotics operation in the Gulf of Guinea that led to the capture of six tonnes of drugs. The Alouette is a fairly easy aircraft to fly, but its instrument panel is not NVG-compatible, so we can't fly with NVGs. Only the loadmaster can be equipped with NVGs, a clear limitation for surveillance/search missions at night.

For surveillance missions, the Alouette III now carries a laptop fitted with an embedded GPS that provides an AIS capability. Lieutenant Nicolas continued: 'Even though our Alouette is not equipped with a radar, the AIS allows us to monitor the flow of ships ahead and around our parent vessel. We also carry a digital camera with an 800mm lens to photograph surface contacts and update the French Navy's various databases.'

The Panther entered service with Flottille 36F of the French Navy in 1995. The Panther has met with considerable success on the export market.

Gap filler

To fill the gap and temporarily replace the last few Alouette IIIs still in service, the French Navy decided to expand the number of Dauphins by leasing an extra 12 AS365N3 aircraft from French company Héli-Union. Called Dauphin N3 FI (Flotte Intérimaire, or interim fleet), these additional aircraft will allow the Navy to retire the Alouette III and to operate a more modern type offering better payload and range. The contract was signed in 2019 and the first helicopter was delivered in early 2021. Six Dauphin N3 FI rotorcraft will eventually be allocated to Flottille 35F and another six to Flottille 34F. Under current plans, the Alouette III will phase out in late 2022.

The first three AS365N3 Dauphin FI helicopters were officially delivered to Flottille 35F in January, February and March 2021. The Dauphin N3 FI is a powerful helicopter that offers aircrews a gratifying level of performance. Flottille 35F's commanding officer, Lieutenant-Commander Lorélie Féraud stated:

Thanks to the Arriel 2C engines, the Dauphin FI has a maximum take-off weight of 4,300kg, compared to 4,000kg for the Dauphin SPI [Secours, Protection et Intervention, or rescue, protection and intervention] and 4,100kg for the Dauphin Pedro. This is a major advantage as we do not have to make a choice between fuel and payload anymore. The N3 FI's performance is far less affected by height or hot weather, and its single engine performance level is a huge step forward for flight safety, especially when landing on hospital platforms surrounded by buildings and obstructions in the middle of city centres.

Different configurations

Due to the Covid crisis, the first five Dauphin N3 FI helicopters were delivered in a temporary configuration that did not offer all the systems and functionalities ordered by the French Navy. The following seven will be delivered with a more comprehensive mission fit. Lieutenant-Commander Lorélie Féraud continued:

Thanks to the adoption of the Euroflir 410 optronics turret, of a GNSS [Global Navigation Satellite System]/NVG-compatible glass cockpit, of the CMA-9000 mission computer that also

A Flottille 36F Panther at its Hyères home base. From 1995 to 2003, the squadron was stationed at Saint-Mandrier, and it moved to Hyères when Saint-Mandrier closed.

Left: Close up of the Euroflir 410 showing its multiple apertures that allow targets to be identified and tracked in a wide range of conditions, day and night.

Below: The quality of the image provided by the Euroflir 410 turret is said to be excellent. Aircrews all seem to be very satisfied with its performance level.

equips the Panther Standard 2, and of a pintle-mounted MAG 58 7.62mm machine gun, the final configuration will offer massively expanded operational capabilities. Aircrews will have at their disposal a tablet/kneepad with a dedicated mission processing software. Moreover, aircraft destined to be flown by detachments at sea will be fitted with a harpoon to secure them on deck during landings and with a late generation Mode 5 Identification Friend or Foe (IFF) that will allow ships to easily identify them. In fact, their equipment level will be close to that of the modernised Panther Standard 2, but with a higher payload and a longer range. They will be able to fly a much larger range of missions than the five early aircraft.

Major changes ahead

Two of the 'new' Flottille 35F aircraft have been singled out to deploy to the Martinique Island, in the French Antilles, to replace the Alouette III of a detachment attached to surveillance frigate *Germinal* (done in September 2021 with one of the early five aircraft) and the Panther of sister-ship *Ventôse* (in mid-2022, with a full-standard variant). The French Navy will then have only one rotary type to support in Fort-de-France, Martinique, thus easing logistics while helping increase operational effectiveness in the area, the replacement of an outdated Alouette III with a Dauphin N3 FI representing a huge step forward in terms of capabilities. Moreover, the Panther brought back to continental France will become available for deployment at sea from other surface combatants. One of Flottille 35F's Dauphin N3 FI helicopters will be allocated to one of the future Bâtiments Ravitailleurs de Forces (BRF, naval forces logistics ships), the first of which, *Jacques Chevalier*, will be accepted into service in 2023. Four of these 31,000-tonne vessels will ultimately replace, at Toulon and Brest, the last three 17,900-tonne Durance-class fleet replenishers (*Marne*, *Var* and *Somme*), which were all commissioned between 1983 and 1990.

Flottille 34F and the Dauphin FI

Over the course of the next two years, Flottille 34F will become a Dauphin-only naval squadron. After 60 years of sterling service, the Alouette III will soon reach the end of its operational career and will be replaced by six Dauphin FI helicopters from DCI/Héli-Union at Lanvéoc-Poulmic. At the time of writing, it was expected that the first aircraft would be delivered to Flottille 34F in December 2021, joining the five NHV aircraft. Two of the Dauphin FI twins are destined to the *Vendémiaire* and *Prairial* detachments, respectively based in Nouméa and Papeete. From 2023, Flottille 34F will keep growing with the planned transfer of two detachments currently allocated to Flottille 36F. These two detachments, which deploy on board surveillance frigates *Nivôse* and *Ventôse* both stationed at Réunion Island, in the Indian Ocean, will convert from the Panther to the Dauphin N3 FI. A further two Flottille 34F Dauphin FI rotorcraft will eventually be stationed at Lanvéoc-Poulmic to provide detachments for the trial ship *Monge* and for the second BRF, the future *Jacques Stosskopf*, which will be commissioned in 2025.

H160M Guépard on the horizon

The Panthers and Dauphins will all be replaced by the future H160M Guépard, a new generation multirole helicopter that will equip the French Navy, the French Army Aviation and the AAE. In terms of weight and payload, the Guépard will slot in between the Panther and the Caïman. The latest technologies have been earmarked for the Guépard, including Blue Edge rotor blades, advanced cockpit and electronic scanning radar arrays mounted in the nose and on the sides of the fuselage to give a 360-degree coverage. This new Thales AirMaster C radar will offer exceptional detection capabilities against naval targets and low probability of interception by enemy radar warning receivers. The French and British ministries of defence have jointly launched the procurement of a lightweight anti-ship missile, which will be used to replace the Sea Skua in Royal Navy service and to arm the H160M in France. This FASGW/ANL (Future Anti-Surface Guided Weapon/Anti-Navire Léger, or light anti-ship) Sea Venom missile will provide the H160M with a robust punch against surface combatants. The Guépard is not due to be equipped with a dunking sonar, however, a major shortcoming that might have to be addressed in the future.

Above: With its wide array of detection equipment (radar, sonar, datalink and self-defence suite), the NH90 is often compared to an embarked maritime patrol aircraft by French Navy officers.

A Flottille 33F Caïman photographed at Lanvéoc-Poulmic between two sorties.

Above: A large percentage of Caïman training is performed in the simulator. Both Hyères and Lanvéoc-Poulmic naval air stations are equipped with a NH90 simulator. Here, the pilot has just performed a simulated landing on board carrier *Charles de Gaulle*.

Right: The Caïman regularly supports French special forces. Here, French Navy commandos fast rope down from a Caïman onto a Rigid Hull Inflatable Boat (RHIB).

Below: On the Aquitaine-class frigates, the vessel and the NH90 detachment share a pooled reserve of 19 MU90 torpedoes.

The Caïman can operate in very strong crosswinds, and its operating envelope when flying to and out of helicopter landing platforms on ships is wider than that of the Westland Lynx. Here, a Flottille 31F Caïman lands on board HMS *Bulwark* during exercise *Corsican Lion* in 2012.

Left: The French Navy has ordered a total of 27 NH90 Caïman helicopters.

Below: The European Navy Radar (ENR) antenna is clearly visible under the fuselage of Caïman s/n 9.

A Flottille 33F Caïman is undergoing maintenance at Lanvéoc-Poulmic. The availability rate of the Caïman has been adversely affected by teething problems, but the situation is now slowly improving.

Above left: The French Navy NH90 Caïman is powered by two RTM322 turbines.

Above right: The Caïman is more than twice heavier than its predecessor, the Lynx.

Caïman s/n 21 will soon leave Hyères for yet another training mission.

The Caïman's main sensor for anti-submarine warfare (ASW) is the Thales Underwater Systems FLASH low-frequency sonar. Here, Flottille 31F technicians install a sonar in the main cabin of a Caïman.

Above left: The classic lines of the faithful Alouette III. When it entered service, the Alouette was one of the most advanced helicopters anywhere.

Above right: A Flottille 34F Alouette III hovering low over the ocean off Brittany.

Left: The SA319 variant of the Alouette III family can be easily identified by its orange emergency flotation gear positioned high along the fuselage. On the SA316, the gear was much lower.

Right: Flottille 35F's permanent detachments are now spread all over the world, from Tahiti, in the vast expanses of the Pacific, to Fort-de-France, in the Caribbean Sea, a distance record for a French unit.

Below: One of Flottille 35F's new SA365N3 Dauphin helicopters of the FI (Flotte Intérimaire, or interim fleet).

Above: The Dauphin is renowned for its ease of maintenance and its large spares inventory available worldwide.

Left: Lieutenant-Commander Lorélie Féraud, Flottille 35F commanding officer, photographed doing her pre-flight checks prior to a mission.

Below: French Navy aircrews and engineers all work together as closely-knit teams.

The French Navy's choice of the Dauphin for its interim helicopter fleet is a low-risk approach. A number of Dauphins were readily available on the secondhand market due to the reduction of the need for offshore helicopters for the oil market.

Above left: The Dauphin is a compact helicopter, with a rather tight main cabin, restricting rescue capabilities to four or five survivors at most.

Above right: A Flottille 35F winchman photographed in the rear cabin of a SA365N3 Dauphin.

Right: Noteworthy is the antenna of the civilian weather radar of this Dauphin N3 FI undergoing maintenance in Flottille 35F's hangar in Hyères.

Chapter 5
Maritime Patrol and Maritime Surveillance

French Navy Atlantique 2, Falcon 50 and Gardian maritime patrol and maritime surveillance aircraft undertake a wide range of blue water and coastal missions, in direct support of French submarine and surface forces and in close cooperation with other agencies.

No fewer than 28 Atlantique 2s have been produced by Dassault Aviation for the French Navy. While other MPAs are derivatives of airliners (Comet for the Nimrod, Electra for the P-3 Orion, Boeing 737 for the P-8 Poseidon), the Atlantic/Atlantique 2 family was specifically designed for over the sea/anti-submarine operations. As a result, the aircraft proves very much at ease at low level over the sea, day and night. Today, two Flottilles, 21F and 23F, remain operational on the type at Lann-Bihoué, near Lorient, in Brittany.

A truly multirole platform

The Atlantique 2 performs a bewildering variety of missions, both over the sea and over land. While it can also perform a wide range of other tasks, including maritime surveillance, traffic interdiction, fishery protection and SAR, its main mission clearly remains ASW with the MU90 torpedo. The aircraft also excels in the anti-ship role with the AM39 Exocet Block 8 missile.

The Atlantic 1 was often used for airborne forward air control missions over land, guiding strikes of Jaguar and Mirage F1 fighters over the vast expanses of the Sahara Desert. Today, the range of the over land missions performed by the Atlantique 2 has been expanded to include wide area surveillance, targeting and kinetic strikes with GBU-12 and GBU-58 laser-guided bombs of the Paveway II family.

Improved Standard 6

Atlantique 2s are now being brought up to the much-improved Standard 6, which offers massively increased operational capabilities. For the French Navy, the progressive admission into service of upgraded Standard 6 Atlantique 2 MPAs represents a major step forward in ASW and anti-ship warfare. The first Standard 6 aircraft was delivered in September 2019.

As a reminder, five Atlantique 2 standards had been flown by the French Navy before the advent of the Standard 6:

- Standards 1 and 2, which both entered service in the early 1990s.
- Standard 3, which appeared in 1995. It introduced the NATO Link 11 datalink that enabled the automatic exchange of data between an Atlantique 2 and friendly aircraft and ships operating on the same L11 network.
- Standard 4, which was fully compatible with the new MU90 Impact torpedo to replace the outdated, US-built Mk 46 torpedo. The Standard 4 entered service in 2006.
- Standard 5/ICAO (International Civil Aviation Organisation) compatibility. Launched in 2012, it covered the adoption of a modernised instrument panel with four multifunction screens, two

flight management systems for the aircraft commander and the co-pilot, and a TCAS (Traffic Collision Avoidance System). By the end of 2018, all 22 remaining aircraft had been brought up to this standard.

The Standard 6 is a much more comprehensive upgrade that is often compared to a weapon system mid-life upgrade.

A highly successful programme

The Standard 6 upgrade was contracted in 2013, and the first upgraded aircraft, M25, made its first flight from Istres in 2016. Over the following three years, an integrated team of specialists drawn from Dassault Aviation, the DGA (the French defence procurement agency) and the French Navy closely cooperated to test the aircraft and detect and iron out all the problems that invariably appear during a complex flight test programme. Commander Thomas Lallouet, a test pilot who was part of the French Navy evaluation team between 2017 and 2019 and who is now the commanding officer of Flottille 21F at Lann-Bihoué, commented:

> Unlike most other defence programmes all over the world, Standard 6 development and trials were conducted on time. Test flights were performed with mixed crews drawn from Dassault Aviation, the DGA and the Navy so that the required amount of expertise was available for the mission. At various stages during the programme, we carried out dedicated flights to check how the aircraft and its combat system behaved under operational stress, exploring the borders of the operational envelope to push the new systems to their design limits. These flights allowed us to ensure that everything worked as advertised, in full compliance with the French Navy's expectations.

This photo clearly shows the Atlantique 2's very wide wingspan. The aircraft is incredibly agile at very low level, a major advantage when tracking and engaging a submarine.

Step by step

The first two Atlantique 2 Standard 6 aircraft, M25 and M28, arrived back at Lann-Bihoué in September 2019. Commander Lallouet continued:

This marked the first step of service entry within the French Navy. Initially stationed in Istres, the Atlantique 2 operational evaluation unit had progressively been expanded to concentrate within one unit all the required expertise and prepare the conversion of Flottille 21F from the Standard 5 to the Standard 6. Flottille 21F would then become the first front-line squadron to operate the new variant. In September 2019, the training of the first Flottille 21F aircrews began. In December 2020, initial operational capability was reached, with five trained crews and three aircraft, M25, M28 and M16. We have now received another two aircraft, M9 and M11, and full operational capability will be achieved in early 2022, with eight fully trained crews and five upgraded aircraft. At that stage, Flottille 21F will be fully operational on the Standard 6 while Flottille 23F will continue flying the Standard 5 until 2023, when it will begin its transition onto the new standard. To summarise, 21F in 2021, and 23F in 2023. The last of the 18 aircraft upgraded to the Standard 6 should be delivered back to the French Navy in 2025, with deliveries continuing until then at the rate of one aircraft every three to four months.

A large array of new systems

The Standard 6 upgrade focused on four main aspects:

- Introduction of the Thales SEARCHMASTER® AESA radar.
- Replacement of the old ASW system by the Système de Traitement Acoustique Numérique (STAN), a new generation digital acoustic processing system that is fully compatible with the latest sonobuoys in production or now being developed.
- Adoption of a MX-20 electro-optical turret for all 18 aircraft to be upgraded to Standard 6.
- Installation of new displays and workstations in the main cabin.

A Standard 6 Atlantique 2 maritime patrol aircraft of Flottille 21F at low-level over the Atlantic Ocean, with the Quiberon Peninsula in the background.

For the casual observer, this could be a rather limited upgrade. In fact, this is a major step forward, as Commander Lallout insisted:

> While a Standard 6 Atlantique 2 might look externally similar to a Standard 5 aircraft, it's an entirely different beast internally. Even though the airframe and the engines are unchanged, the modernisation of the weapon system proves to be a change similar to the switch from the Super Étendard to the Rafale for the fast jet community, or from the Lynx to the NH90 Caïman for our rotary wing colleagues. It's not just new screens and new sensors. It's a complete package that, on top of the systems, induces a doctrinal revolution, with new tactics adapted to the new capabilities. In some ways, we have to learn again how to perform the mission, even though basic skills remain unaltered.

New radar

The advent of the SEARCHMASTER radar helped propel the Atlantique into modernity. This new radar has benefited from technology transfers from the Rafale's AESA radar. While the Rafale's RBE2 radar relies solely on electronic scanning, the SEARCHMASTER relies on a double mechanical/electronic scanning to guarantee an optimal rate of scanning for each search sweep, enabling small, pinpoint targets to be tracked with outstanding accuracy. At the request of the French Navy, a high resolution ISAR (Inverse Synthetic Aperture Radar) mode was adopted for the SEARCHMASTER to identify ships at stand-off ranges. A specific mode to track submarine periscopes in high sea states has also been developed. Derived from a fighter radar, the SEARCHMASTER offers specific modes to detect and track airborne targets and identify them thanks to an embedded IFF interrogator. This is a crucial advantage for flight safety, the Atlantique crew now being able to precisely know the position of other MPAs in the area and, even more importantly, of ASW helicopters involved in the search of a submarine. The SEARCHMASTER offers considerably expanded detection ranges. It is a very automated radar set with a software that helps operators exploit to the full its endless capabilities.

Above left: Atlantique 2 s/n M16 displays the radome of its SEARCHMASTER® AESA (Active Electronically Scanned Array) radar in the extended position.

Above right: Egyptian Gowind frigate *El Fateh* photographed from an Atlantique 2 in 2017. *El Fateh* was built in Lorient shipyard, a few kilometres away from Lann-Bihoué Naval Air Station.

STAN and sonobuoys

With the STAN and its new expendable sonobuoys, the Atlantique 2 Standard 6 can detect submarines on an enlarged bandwidth and counter the most recent and silent threats.

To replace ageing analogue types (that remain operational with Standard 5 aircraft), a whole new generation of foreign digital sonobuoys has been adopted by the French Navy for the Standard 6 fleet:

- A new type of passive directional sonobuoy with an embedded GPS and a wider range of operating frequencies than the previous passive DIFAR (DIrectional Frequency Analysis and Recording).
- New buoys optimised for very low frequencies for use against the latest generation of stealthy submarines.

Left: The Standard 6's MX™-20 EO turret can easily been seen under the fuselage of Atlantique 2 M16.

Below: The Standard 6 is fitted with an aerodynamic fairing under the nose, which replicates the shape of the Tango FLIR that was removed during the upgrade programme.

- A multi-static sonobuoy that generates a very powerful active sonar beam that will be reflected by a submerged submarine and will bounce back to be detected by a field of passive buoys carefully positioned to interdict a wide area. It can also be used like a traditional, high power active buoy.

Flottille 23F Standard 5 Atlantique 2s still rely on older types of sonobuoys that still prove effective even though they are now ageing :

- DICASS (DIrectional Command Activated Sonobuoy System) active omnidirectional.
- LOFAR (LOw Frequency And Recording) passive wide band.
- The aforementioned DIFAR.

As part of NATO interoperability, the Standard 6 is capable of operating with the latest foreign sonobuoys and Flottille 21F aircrews train to receive and process data from other types of sonobuoys than those in service with the French Navy. The obvious goal is to ensure that an Atlantique 2 can receive and process information from a sonobuoy barrage that has been laid by another, allied MPA.

Thanks to the new digital sonobuoy, the quality of data processing carried out by the STAN, and the know-how of French acoustic operators, detection ranges against the latest generation of submarines have been significantly improved compared with un-modernised Atlantique 2s. It is a true revolution. No ranges can be revealed, but the broad smiles on the faces of the interviewed officers were a clear indication of the huge leap forward that has just been made.

EO turret

As part of an urgent operational requirement, three Standard 5 aircraft had been brought up to an interim standard called 'Fox' that allowed them to be equipped with a WESCAM MX™-20D electro-optical turret that offered massively expanded capabilities compared to those of the Atlantique 2's original Tango FLIR. While the Tango's outdated infrared sensor generates a monochrome image, the MX-20D is fitted with a full assortment of high-resolution TV and IR sensors. Even more impressive is the fact that the TV and IR images can be overlaid to work in difficult conditions, at sunrise or sunset for example.

Atlantique 2 M16 breaks away to show its opened weapon bay. An orange-painted air-droppable SAR kit is always carried by Atlantiques during training and operational missions, as they always stand ready to assist any ship or person when airborne.

Above: The MX-20 EO turret under the Atlantique 2's fuselage is directly pointed at the Flottille 24F Falcon 50 photo ship.

Left: French Navy Atlantique 2s specialise in anti-ship and ASW. They also protect nuclear strategic submarines that go in and out of their Ile Longue base, near Brest.

While the MX-20D was an optional fit for the Standard 5 'Fox', it is permanently fitted to the rear of Standard 6 aircraft at the expense of an 18-tube sonobuoy dispenser. It should be noted that a further 18 sonobuoys can now be carried internally, however, thus offsetting the reduction caused by the adoption of the MX-20 turret.

Depending on the missions to be carried out, two types of turrets of the MX-20 family can be mounted on any of the Standard 6 aircraft:

- MX-20D, with the full spectrum of day/night functionalities, an infrared pointer and a laser designation capability to guide GBU-12 and GBU-58 laser-guided bombs.
- MX-20HD, with the same day/night sensors, but without the laser designation capability.

With the western tip of the island of Belle-Ile-en-Mer in the background, Atlantique 2 Standard 6 M16 heads towards the high seas for yet another mission.

This choice was made to minimise procurement and operating costs but will probably reduce operational flexibility. The Tango FLIR turrets that were installed under the nose of the aircraft are removed in the course of the upgrade and replaced with an aerodynamical fairing to maintain stability in yaw, and weights are fitted in the nose to preserve weight and balance.

New touchscreen displays

The upgrade of the main cabin gave way to the introduction of new workstations. The Deputy Commander of Flottille 21F stated:

> Our operators switched from monochrome circular displays to large, colour touchscreens. This is a huge step forwards that significantly reduces the operators' workload and ameliorates their understanding of the evolving tactical situation. But that's not the only advantage. Over the years, a number of systems had been added to the aircraft. Such is the case, for example, of the AIS, the Automatic Identification System that reveals the identity of a ship, in the same way as an aircraft transponder or IFF. On the Standard 5, the AIS was available on a laptop and the operators had to mentally correlate the radar image on their monochrome display with what they were seeing on their laptop screen. Now, our operators and tactic specialists have directly access to all AIS data on their displays. The AIS situation can even be overlaid on the radar display to obtain an unambiguous, fused AIS/radar image. Pretty neat. The French Navy's photographic database of ships that was previously available on a laptop only is now fully embedded into the aircraft's weapon system.

The aircraft's communication suite and its ARAR-13 electronic support measure system have not been modernised during the Standard 5 to Standard 6 upgrade. As a result, the workstations of the radio and electronic warfare operators have not been upgraded either.

Enhanced tactics

Standard 6 offers formidable operational capabilities to the French Navy, and aircrews spare no effort to refine their offensive anti-ship and ASW tactics. A new tactical manual has been written from scratch. The Deputy Commander continued:

> We are constantly trying to innovate and improve our tactics. What we need to avoid is to do the same with the new equipment as we did with the un-modernised aircraft. For example, for anti-ship missions, our new sensors allow us to operate at a higher altitude, from further away, over a much larger area. But it is not only a question of pure detection range. We are less vulnerable because the range of our sensors gives us the opportunity to be less conspicuous while investigating contacts from considerable distances, without our presence being necessarily detected and without engaging the missile defence zone of hostile surface combatants.
>
> The progress made is not only linked to the adoption of the STAN and of the new sonobuoys as part of the switch from analogue to digital technology. The carefully designed workstations, with their refined ergonomics, also contribute to better operational capabilities because their screens are newer, with an immensely improved resolution. The acoustic specialists now have a better understanding of the underwater situation as they can select many frequencies on their screens simultaneously. Colour displays are also a major step forward because colour pixels that start to form a line will be more easily spotted than colourless dots on a low-resolution monochrome screen.

Above left: A Flottille 23F Standard 5 Atlantique 2 is being pushed back towards its parking spot at Lann-Bihoué.

Above right: Flottille 23F Atlantique 2 M27 undergoing post flight inspection by a team of engineers. Flottilles 21F and 23F are co-located at Lann-Bihoué.

Right: Atlantique 2 M5 being refuelled at its Lann-Bihoué home base. Atlantique 2s very rarely adorn squadron markings.

Below: Atlantique 2 M27 comes in to land at Lann-Bihoué. Most sorties end up with a few touch-and-goes to give the two pilots the opportunity to hone their landing skills.

Crew training

Each Atlantique 2 crew is set up for a cycle of three to four years. It is composed of 14 crew members: a pilot/captain, a co-pilot, two flight engineers, a tactical coordinator, three radar operators/navigators, three radio/electronic warfare operators and three acoustic specialists to remotely operate the sonobuoys. Until the advent of the Standard 6, aircrews used to be swapped around Flottilles 21F and 23F, with individuals being posted from one to the other squadron according to the needs of the respective units. This situation has changed, and aircrews trained on the Standard 6 now remain with Flottille 21F until further notice, as they are not allowed to man a Standard 5 aircraft anymore.

It takes only three months for an experienced Standard 5 crew to complete its conversion onto the new Standard 6, with the training course focusing on system architecture, emergency procedures, basic tactics and advanced operational doctrine. For ab-initio aircrews straight out of basic training school, the process is considerably longer and is typically spread over nine to 12 months. Twenty 21F and 23F crews will eventually be operational on the Standard 6 at the end of a massive conversion and training effort.

New capabilities planned for the near future

While it is likely that the Standard 6 will be the last major upgrade for the Atlantique 2 before it is withdrawn from use around 2035, additional ameliorations are already being planned to further increase its operational capabilities. The aircraft should receive the new joint, multinational Link 22 datalink. The L22 will be more robust than the current L11, with tremendously improved data transfer capabilities. It will also prove much more resistant to jamming and intrusion.

At the end of their low-level sorties over the sea, the Atlantique 2s are cleaned with high-pressure fresh water in an effort to keep corrosion under control.

Above: An Atlantique 2 on short final at Lann-Bihoué. The visibility from the forward observation window is just outstanding. It is not manned in the landing circuit, however.

Right: Flares fired from the rear left launcher of an Atlantique 2. The photo was taken from the rear left bubble window.

Below: The Atlantic/Atlantique 2 family has served well the French Navy for nearly 60 years.

Commander Lallout explained: 'The integration of the L22 is expected to begin in 2023 and I think that in-flight trials will be rapidly expedited. We will have to loan one of our aircraft to Dassault Aviation for a few months for the trial programme.'

From 2025, new French-designed and French-built sonobuoys will enter service on the Atlantique 2 Standard 6 to replace the Canadian or US types currently in service. Conceived by Thales, one of the world leaders in sonar technology, they will give the French industry and the French Armed Forces a much-needed technological and strategic autonomy in that highly sensitive field. These SonoFlash buoys will also equip the Caïman helicopters.

Left: Colour and smoke marine markers have been dropped into the ocean during a SAR exercise. The visibility from the rear bubble window is just outstanding.

Below: French Navy engineers are busy changing a Rolls-Royce Tyne turbine. This engine, which also powers the Transall C-160, is renowned for its reliability.

Flottille 24F Falcon 50 MSAs

For coast guard-type missions, Flottille 24F, at Lann-Bihoué, operates eight Falcon 50 missionised business jets split into four Falcon 50Mi (maritime intervention) and four Falcon 50 MSi (maritime surveillance and intervention) variants. The four Mi aircraft, construction numbers 7, 30, 36 and 132, were procured on the second-hand market and introduced in the early 2000s while their four brethren, nos 5, 27, 34 and 78, are ex-AAE VVIP aircraft that have been modified and transferred back to the French Navy between 2014 and 2016. All these aircraft specialise in the maritime surveillance role and carry out a large range of missions, including SAR, maritime approaches protection, drug interdiction, illegal traffic and immigration control, fisheries protection, pollution control/environmental protection, fire range safety, and surveillance of national borders and sensitive areas.

Extensive modifications were required to transform the business jets into maritime surveillance aircraft. They all received large side windows, a nose-mounted Ocean Master 100 radar, a Chlio FLIR turret that could retract into the rear fuselage and dedicated workstations in the main cabin for the navigator/radar operator and the radio operator. The initial Mi variant was equipped from the start with a large hatch/release door under the forward fuselage to drop large survival kits. The Mi can also drop a special container that is used for logistics missions, giving the squadron the capability to deliver from the air small spare parts or critical equipment to a ship at sea. The MSi was initially delivered in an interim standard that was incapable of dropping SAR kits. It was soon decided to address the shortcoming, however, and the aircraft has been modified with a drop hatch, albeit smaller than that of the Mi. Both variants are flown by two pilots, a tactical situation operator, a radio operator, and a radar operator/navigator.

The aircraft has proved to be very effective in French Navy service, performing a wide range of missions from naval air stations and air bases in France and abroad. Lieutenant-Commander Boris Wertenberg, Flottille 24F's commanding officer, explained: 'Even though the aircraft is ageing,

The Atlantique 2's upgraded instrument panel was introduced on the Standard 5. It comprises four multifunction screens.

availability remains excellent thanks to the Falcon's rugged airframe and strong engines. Corrosion, a common issue for aircraft that fly low over the sea, is kept under tight control. Thankfully, Dassault Aviation aircraft are renowned for their corrosion protection and for the uncompromising quality of the metal alloys chosen for their airframes.'

Gardians of the Pacific

The Gardian, a dedicated maritime surveillance variant of the Falcon 20/200 family, was inducted into French Navy service in the early 1980s to replace outdated P2V-7 Neptunes that carried out surveillance and SAR missions in the Pacific. The five jets were initially split between Escadrilles 9S and 12S, respectively based in Nouméa (New Caledonia) and Papeete (Tahiti) but have been flown by Flottille 25F since September 2000 from the same two bases. Four aircraft, equally split between the two bases, are in service at any given time, with the fifth undergoing depot-level maintenance. They are flown by a crew of six: two pilots, a flight engineer, a radio operator, and two radar operators/navigators.

Thanks to their Varan radar, observation windows and drop hatch, the Gardians perform the whole spectrum of maritime SAR and surveillance missions, helping maintain French sovereignty over a huge exclusive economic zone in close cooperation with French Navy and Gendarmerie Nationale surface vessels.

Albatros in 2025

In late 2020, an order for an initial batch of seven Albatroses was announced by the French Navy. Eventually, 12 will be purchased to replace the five Gardians and the eight Falcon 50M jets. Compared to the current aircraft, the Albatros will provide considerably expanded operational capabilities and a much more comfortable working environment for the aircrews. Detection capabilities will be massively improved via the adoption of the SEARCHMASTER AESA radar and of the Euroflir 410 EO system. The aircraft, a variant of the Falcon 2000LXS business jet, will offer significantly increased range and time on station. Compared to the Gardian and to the Falcon 50M, the Albatros is a bigger and much more modern aircraft with substantially better operational performance. Its cruise speed will be slightly higher and its endurance significantly longer: it will be able to remain on station 2hr 45min at 1,200nm (2,222km) from its base against 1hr 30min at 1,000nm (1,852km) for a Falcon 50M.

A comprehensive flight test programme will be undertaken from 2024, and the first three Albatroses should be delivered to the French Navy in 2025. As a stop gap measure, five Flottille 24F Falcons, the four Mi aircraft and a single MSi variant, are currently being upgraded with a the Euroflir 410 EO turret, a new generation system that offers considerably increased capabilities over the outdated Chlio.

For opportunity reconnaissance missions, Single-Lens Reflex (SLR) cameras with powerful lenses are carried. The operator shoots through a flat window. Images produced in such a way are incredibly good, even at long distances.

Above left: The main cabin of a Standard 6 Atlantique 2, as seen from the rear of the aircraft. The crew member shown in the foreground is an acoustic operator in charge of managing the sonobuoys.

Above right: The Atlantique 2's main cabin, looking from the front to the rear. The workstation of the radio operator in the foreground has not been upgraded when the aircraft was modernised up to Standard 6.

Above left: The Standard 6 aircraft are equipped with the latest generation of touch screen colour displays.

Above right: This photo taken on the ground shows an Atlantique 2 in two different wavelengths. The MX-20 turret is equipped with very powerful sensors.

Large numbers of sonobuoys are readily available at Lann-Bihoué. They could be rapidly loaded onto the Atlantique 2s, should the need arise.

This Standard 6 Atlantique 2 overflies an offshore wind turbine off Brittany.

A pair of GBU-12 Paveway II laser-guided bombs about to be loaded onto an Atlantique 2.

A team of armourers load a GBU-12 laser-guided bomb into the cavernous weapon bay of an Atlantique 2 at Lann-Bihoué.

Above left: The GBU-12 has been used operationally by the Atlantique 2 community in the Sahara against terrorist groups.

Above right: Sonobuoys and marine markers in their dispensers on board an Atlantique 2.

Above left: The MU90 is the Atlantique 2's weapon of choice against submarines. The training rounds are orange-painted.

Above right: The MU90 is a much bigger and heavier weapon than the Mk 46 torpedo it has replaced. It is faster, deeper diving, offers a much longer range and can defeat the thickest submarine hulls.

Flottille 24F Falcon 50MSi s/n 78, photographed at Lann-Bihoué between two sorties.

Right: A Falcon 50Mi (in the foreground) and a Falcon 50MSi share Flottille 24F's main hangar in Lann-Bihoué. Externally, the two variants are very similar.

Below: The beautiful lines of Falcon 50MSi s/n 5 high over a solid cloud layer.

This Flottille 24F Falcon 50 deploys its landing gear at high level...just for the photo.

The Falcon offers excellent high-altitude performance. It could even outclimb a Super Étendard.

Above: Falcon MSi s/n 5 breaks away at a high level to demonstrate its agility.

Below: Even though the Falcon 50M is an ageing design, its flight deck looks quite modern, with large multifunction displays.

Chapter 6
SAR Missions

The French Naval Aviation plays a crucial role providing SAR coverage alongside French coastlines, in continental France and in the French overseas territories.

In France, a large number of rotary assets spread all over the country (including the French overseas territories) are dedicated to offshore and mountain SAR. They include Sécurité Civile and Gendarmerie EC145 helicopters, AAE Pumas and Caracals and French Navy Dauphins and Caïmans. All these helicopters are carefully positioned to provide overlapping capabilities. They are all supported by French Navy Falcon 50 and Gardian maritime patrol aircraft allocated to Flottille 24F at Lann-Bihoué, and Flottille 25F at Papeete and Nouméa (New Caledonia), respectively.

A long tradition of SAR at sea

The French Navy has long operated both helicopters and fixed-wing aircraft in the SAR role. Until its retirement in 2010, the Super Frelon was the iconic SAR aircraft in France. It flew countless SAR missions off Brittany and in the Mediterranean, often in treacherous conditions, at night and in bad weather. In 2010, it was temporarily replaced by a pair of EC225 helicopters that were ultimately transferred to the AAE, leaving the heavy SAR role to the NH90 Caïman. Today, Flottille 35F SA365N Dauphin SPI (Secours, Protection et Intervention, or rescue, protection and intervention) and Flottille 33F Caïman Marine helicopters supported by Falcon 50M and Gardian maritime surveillance aircraft form the backbone of the French Navy rescue force.

A single Caïman is based in Cherbourg, while another stands ready to take off from Lanvéoc-Poulmic. Three Dauphins are maintained at short readiness from their bases in Le Touquet, La Rochelle and Hyères. While Sécurité Civile EC145 helicopters mainly operate in the coastal environment, remaining close to the shore, French Navy Caïmans and Dauphins routinely perform longer-range rescues, operating far from land to pick up wounded or critically ill persons from a ship, or pluck survivors from the sea. French Navy helicopters also regularly perform SAR missions from their mother ships at sea during blue-water operations, when taking part in deployments or in exercises.

Caïman heavy SAR asset

For SAR missions, the Caïman is flown by a crew of four: pilot, tactical coordinator, sensor operator (Senso) who doubles as a winchman, and rescue diver. Usually, a doctor and a nurse are taken on board to provide offshore emergency medical assistance. In case of a fire, a chemical hazard or a breached hull with water flooding a ship, specialised marine emergency response teams can be airlifted in to assist the vessel's crew with dedicated, air-transportable, compact, lightweight firefighting or water-pumping equipment. These teams are strategically located around the country.

Lieutenant-Commander Stéphane is a highly experienced pilot with over 5,000 flying hours to his credit. As such, he is ideally qualified to describe the outstanding capabilities offered by the NH90 in the SAR role:

Compared to the Super Frelon, the Caïman offers considerably expanded operational capabilities. It can scramble and operate in more severe weather conditions thanks to its four-axis autopilot, which allows us to take off with very low ceiling and visibility. Its main and tail rotors, its air intakes, its windscreen and its tail plane are all de-iced. We can now operate in icing conditions that would have prevented a Super Frelon from taking off. During winching, the NH90 has a much larger operating envelope. We do not have to face all the time into wind anymore as the Caïman will accept much stronger cross winds. The only problem is that the Caïman hovers with a five-degree nose up attitude during winching, which restricts somewhat forward visibility. The NH90's flight controls are much more reactive than those of the Super Frelon. On the Super Frelon, when you pushed the stick forward, the helicopter would respond about one second later. Like the Lynx, the NH90 is fitted with a rigid rotor, and it instantly reacts to any control input.

Compared to its predecessor, the Caïman cruises at 160kts instead of 135kts, a significant improvement for SAR missions, which cuts down the amount of time needed to reach a ship. Its endurance is better too, 3hr instead of 2hr 45min. That means we can remain on station for 1hr 30min at the extreme west of our area of responsibility when taking off from Cherbourg.

SAR missions supported by the Falcon 50

When a long-range SAR mission is launched, a French Navy maritime surveillance aircraft is often sent ahead of the helicopter to perform the on-scene commander role. During such SAR missions, the Falcon 50s and the Gardians do play a crucial role, helping accurately locate the ship before the helicopter reaches the area. Instructions can also be given to the ship's captain in advance, asking him to take a given route that will prove more appropriate for winching. As a result, no time is lost when the helicopter arrives on station.

If required, the Falcon 50 can also deliver survival kits from the air. Up to eight air-droppable life-rafts can be simultaneously carried in the cabin of a Falcon 50 Mi, each large enough to accommodate either ten or 25 persons depending on the type. However, the normal load for routine missions is one or two kits only. When assuming SAR alert, the Falcons are generally fitted with a load of six, 3x25 and 3x10, enough for 105 survivors. Prior to release, the bulky life-rafts have to be

The NH90 Caïman of the Cherbourg-based SAR detachment of Flottille 33F stands ready to take off to provide a heavy SAR asset in the Channel. As part of the Franco-British cooperation, the detachment routinely intervenes in the Channel Islands.

manhandled by the flight engineer and the radio operator thanks to a winch mounted on a rail on the cabin roof. The Falcon 50 MSi variant can carry up to ten AM4 SAR kits, each with a nine-person dinghy. While, in the Mi, the drop is remotely initiated at the flick of a switch by the pilots, or manually by the flight engineer, the release is manually triggered by an operator in the MSi.

In the Pacific

In the Pacific, two Flottille 35F Dauphin N3+ helicopters based in Tahiti specialise in the SAR role and routinely cooperate with Flottille 25F Gardians during long-range SAR missions in French Polynesia. They are all tasked by the Tahiti Rescue Coordination Centre. The Dauphins also stand ready to fight bush and forest fires with Bambi buckets.

The Gardians are also routinely tasked to perform urgent medical evacuations from isolated French communities in the Pacific, flying critical patients for treatment from remote islands to regional hospitals in Tahiti or Nouméa. For this mission, the aircraft can carry a fully medicalised stretcher and a medical team. The Gardian is a small aircraft, however, and working conditions are rather cramped for the doctor and nurse. In this respect too, the arrival of the Falcon 50, and then of the Albatros will be major steps forward.

Changes to be introduced for the SAR force

At the time of writing, the French Navy was in the middle of a major reorganisation of its SAR rotary force. As part of a contractor owned/military operated programme, six H160 helicopters will be flown by French Navy personnel. The H160 fits nicely between the Dauphin and the Caïman in terms of size and capabilities (range and payload/number of survivors). Flottille 32F will be recreated at Lanvéoc-Poulmic in 2022 to operate these aircraft. It will become fully operational on the new type in 2023, taking over SAR missions in continental France from bases at Lanvéoc-Poulmic, Cherbourg and Hyères. This will allow the NH90 detachment in Cherbourg to convert from the NH90 to the H160, helping the Caïman force concentrate on high-end combat missions. However, the NH90 will continue to be available for SAR missions from Lanvéoc-Poulmic should a higher capacity helicopter with a longer range be required. Similarly, the Dauphin that will be replaced with an H160 at Hyères will also become available for other missions. The six H160 provided by the civilian industry will all be eventually supplanted by military owned H160M Guépards once the new type is firmly in service.

The French Navy Caïman in Cherbourg is maintained at a high level of readiness, ready to scramble in less than 20 minutes during 'business hours' and under 60 minutes during off-hour duty.

Above left: The Caïman winchman checks the winch prior to a major SAR exercise in Cherbourg harbour.

Above right: Rescue equipment is lowered onto a ship during a large-scale SAR exercise.

Above left: A rescue diver is winched back on board the Caïman. These divers are trained to very high standard and can undertake underwater investigations to ensure that nobody is trapped under an overturned sailboat, for example.

Above right: This rescue diver climbs back on board the Caïman. Even though the French Armed Forces have purchased British-made Alpha helmets for their helicopter aircrews, rescue divers continue using their old helmets, as the British one is deemed too fragile for their missions.

Below left: Thumb up! The exercise has been a total success.

Below right: A Dauphin SPI (Secours, Protection, Intervention, or Rescue, Protection, Intervention) taxies out at Hyères prior to a training sortie. Flottille 35F Dauphin SPI helicopters are stationed at Hyères, Le Touquet and La Rochelle.

Above: Most of the time, the Dauphin SPI helicopters are launched to rescue a wounded sailor on board a trawler, or to carry out a search prior to recovering a missing wind surfer.

Left: One of the civilian-owned/military-operated Dauphin N3 helicopters that recently entered service with the French Navy is seen here recovering a life-guard during an exercise in the Mediterranean Sea.

A rescue diver oversees the winching of a special stretcher specifically designed to rescue a baby.

This Flottille 35F Dauphin N3 seems to dwarf the rescue launch during a rescue/winching exercise.

Above left: A Flottille 24F Falcon 50Mi undergoing maintenance at Lann-Bihoué between two sorties.

Above right: The massive SAR kits in service with the first four Falcon Mi variants delivered to the French Navy, each large enough to accommodate either 10 or 25 persons depending on the type of life-raft packed in the kit.

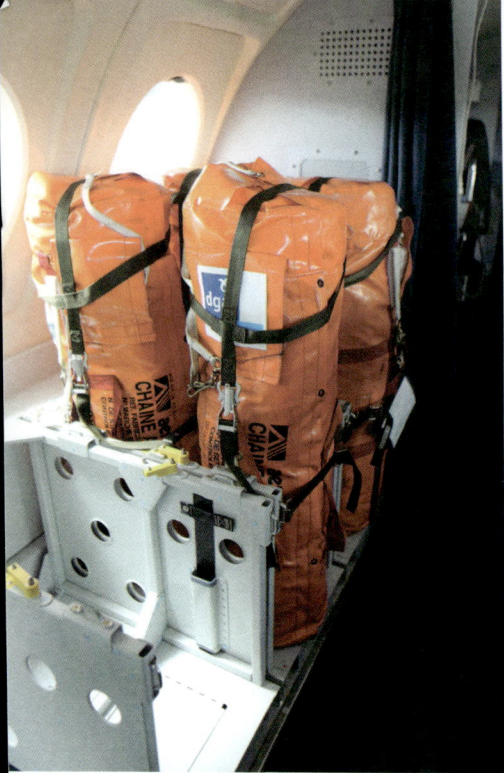

Above: One of Flottille 24F's Falcon 50s sits in its hangar at Lann-Bihoué in May 2021.

Left: Four of the compact AM4 SAR kits, each with a nine-person dinghy, carried by the Falcon 50 MSi.

Below: A Falcon 50MSi at high level. The Falcon 50's speed is its main advantage for SAR missions. SAR coverage for the Channel, the Atlantic Ocean and the Mediterranean Sea is provided from Lann-Bihoué.